Praise for *Sweet Memories*

"Discover the extraordinary life of J. Eugene Salomon, a man whose journey through three countries is as captivating as it is inspiring. From the ravages of the Spanish Civil War, which left his once-wealthy family in ruins, to enduring the horror of German planes attacking the streets of his beloved Asturias, Salomon's early years forged in him an unyielding resilience and determination to succeed.

Now, after '94 years of coincidences', as he describes his life, Salomon continues to share his wealth of knowledge as a revered Chess Master and successful businessman, advising companies and shaping their futures. In his profound autobiography, he unveils the secrets behind his remarkable achievements, while also revealing the immeasurable impact of love, family, and friendship on his life. Join us in celebrating the indomitable spirit of J. Eugene Salomon—a true testament to the triumph of the human spirit and the enduring power of compassion and perseverance.

In this heartfelt tribute, I extend my deepest gratitude to Eugenio, not only for sharing his remarkable journey, but for the incredible person he is and the lasting legacy he has created."

— Javier J. Zulueta, MD, PhD, Professor of Medicine
Icahn School of Medicine at Mount Sinai, New York, NY

"*Sweet Memories* is a beautiful piece of writing reminding all readers that the moving moments of life and chess are metaphorical, and quite possibly, divinely orchestrated. Salomon's rich story is filled with all that makes us human and all that makes us divine. Bravo!"

— Maria Lopez Twena,
Creator of *MariVi the Master Navigator* Series

"An amazing life story, including a lifelong love of chess and family. Congratulations, mazel tov, on weaving together all the stories of our far-flung family. We send you our love and gratitude for writing this book."

— Annette Woolf, Gene's cousin

"Few can have led such a rich and fulfilling life as Gene Salomon. *Sweet Memories* enchantingly charts a life which saw early success on the chessboard and the opportunity to play against the legendary Alekhine. Gene emigrated from Spain to Cuba and then New Jersey, where he really did experience the American dream: family, a successful corporate career and yet more success on his beloved 64 squares."

—Richard Palliser, IM and Editor of *CHESS* magazine (London)

"A great ode to the Salomon family. This book makes readers feel as if they are having a relaxing chat with an old friend discussing the Salomon family history. The details fill in the story like leaves on the family tree and explain how the game of chess has interwoven throughout their lives."

— Mark Capron, Editor of *The Chess Journalist*

Sweet Memories

Family, Friends, Chess, and Sugar

J. Eugene Salomon
with Diane S. Dahl

Copyright © 2023 by J. Eugene Salomon and Diane S. Dahl

All rights reserved. No part of this book may be reproduced, distributed, or transmitted in any form or by any means, including photocopying, recording, or other electronic or mechanical methods, without the prior written permission of the authors, except in the case of brief quotations embodied in critical reviews and certain other noncommercial uses permitted by copyright law.

Adapted from *Jugando en el tablero de la vida*
by J. Eugene Salomon and Javier Cordero

Some names and identifying details have been changed to protect the privacy of individuals.

Published by SFB Multimedia Publishers

To contact the authors, email sweetmemoriessalomon@gmail.com

ISBN 979-8-9885583-0-9 (paperback)
ISBN 979-8-9885583-1-6 (ebook)

Edited by Andrea Vanryken
Book cover design by Joseph Schwartz
Book interior design by Glenn, www.fiverr.com/sarco2000/

Printed in the United States of America

This book is dedicated to my wonderful wife, Bea, just ahead of our 62nd anniversary, and to our beloved family, the children and grandchildren who are our legacy. Thank you all for your love, patience, and understanding. You have given me so many sweet memories, and I cherish them all.

J. Eugene Salomon

Contents

Foreword xi
Chapter 1: My Parents and their Families 1
Chapter 2: Family Life and War through the Eyes of a Child 23
Chapter 3: My Intense Chess Life 41
Chapter 4: A New Life in Cuba 57
Chapter 5: Making My Way 73
Chapter 6: The American Dream 87
Chapter 7: New Jersey, My Parents, and the NJ Open 107
Chapter 8: The Foundations of a Life 117
Chapter 9: The End of My Career as a Corporate Executive 125
Chapter 10: The Consultant Years 139
Chapter 11: The End of my Competitive Chess Life 143
Chapter 12: 24 Years of Life after 70 149
Chapter 13: Miguel Angel Nepomuceno 165
Chapter 14: Lifelong Friendships 173
Chapter 15: Our Family Tree and Family Ties 181
Epilogue: Sweet Reality & Sweet Dreams 199
Appendix A: How I Became A Grandmaster in Sugar 203
Appendix B: US Chess Federation Life Master at Age 70, Chess Writer at 89 217
Acknowledgments 223
About the Authors 227

Author's Note

This book was born when my father, Robert Salomon Schwarz, then living with me in Havana, Cuba, in 1958, gave me a copy of his memoirs, written in Spanish. During his life (from his birth in Metz, Germany in 1895, to his death in Madrid, Spain, through 1968) my father was a witness to the First World War, the Spanish Civil War, the Second World War, the Batista "coup d'état," and the Cuban Revolution.

In 2011, my son Henry and I translated his book and published it as an e-book for the family under his title: *Walking and Wondering: Living Under the Sign of the Cross in the Shadow of the Swastika* (copyright 2011 by The Salomon Family). It was a labor of love.

In 2014, with co-authors Wayne Conover and Steve Pozarek, I published *40 Years of Friendship: 100 Games of Chess* as an e-book, available in the *Forward Chess* format. In 2016, Javier Cordero published parts of that book on his historical chess website.

In 2017, I was honored by the well-known historian/writer Miguel Angel Nepomuceno with an interview for his chess column at *Zenda/libros* in Spain. His series of five articles was published under the title "*De Alekhine a Kasparov-Eugenio Salomon Rugarcía o como jugar a la ciega en el tablero de la vida.*" In a way, that interview resulted in my becoming a writer…at age eighty-nine!

In 2022, with the help of my co-author, Javier Cordero, Chessy Editorial of Spain published my chess biography: *Jugando en el tablero de la vida.*

In 2023, before my ninety-fifth birthday, I hope to see this family history book published.

Translating, editing, and adapting the book so that it blends seamlessly with my father's story was a difficult task. As one of the many coincidences of my life, I found an exceptional bilingual writer, Diane Dahl, willing to take on the challenge.

I hope that my readers find the life of my father and his Salomon Schwarz and Salomon Rugarcía heritage inspirational.

J. Eugene Salomon

Co-Author's Note

I have known the Salomon family since Gene's son, Henry, and I were in middle school together forty-five years ago. While dropping something off at their house, Gene, then age ninety-three, told me he wanted to translate his book from Spanish into English, but the first two people he asked were unavailable. After a few minutes, I guess he remembered that I speak Spanish and asked if I wanted to do it. Having absolutely no idea what I was getting myself into, I said, "Sure!" I had just retired from the education world and was ready for something new.

What a wild ride this has been! After using my Spanish in a school setting for thirty years, I was excited for the challenge of translating something that had nothing to do with teaching. I got my wish. The focus of the book was Gene's eight decades of chess and life across three countries. Gene realized that I knew close to nothing about chess, was very patient, and was even convinced that with his tutelage, I'd be playing in no time. (Nope—sorry, Gene.)

Working with Gene for the last two years has been a true pleasure; he is extremely intelligent, well-spoken, and has a great sense of humor. You might think a man of his age might have trouble remembering the details of ninety-four years, but not him—he's still sharper than most of the people I know. He has taught me so much about Spanish and European history, politics, and geography, the inner workings of the sugar industry, pre-Castro Cuba, and tons of new Spanish vocabulary. The stories he has told me about his family's experiences are remarkable, and the respect and admiration he holds for his father is truly touching.

But what stood out most for me about Gene was his absolute dedication to his family and to family unity, which he attributes to his father's example. At age ninety-four, Gene is still in contact with many of the living members of his family, has orchestrated large-scale family reunions, and has continued to facilitate his children's and grandchildren's contact with their second and third cousins in Spain. Gene regularly declares that of all the things he is proud of in life, his greatest treasure is his four children and seven grandchildren. They are an amazing family. I know Gene is very excited to be telling their story, and I am proud to have helped him do it.

I enjoyed the process immensely. When we first embarked on this adventure, Gene said he hoped that this might be the start of a new career for me in translating and editing. He might be right. Through Gene, I have met the president of the Chess Journalists of America, Joshua Anderson, who is writing a chess-related book. Although I still don't play chess, not only am I now helping to edit Joshua's book and the CJA newsletter, but I've also just been asked to be a judge for their annual chess journalism awards.

> *Mil gracias, Gene, por tu paciencia y confianza en mí— me has introducido realmente a un mundo completamente nuevo a través de nuestra "Magnum Opus". Eres un hombre de categoría, y es un privilegio conocerte y trabajar contigo en este libro.*
>
> *Un abrazo muy fuerte, Diane*

I dedicate my work on this book to my wonderful husband of thirty years, Dee, and our two amazing daughters, Elizabeth and Victoria. You three are my world and have given me all of my life's sweetest memories.

Diane S. Dahl

Foreword

Agatha Christie used to say that remembering is one of the pleasurable compensations of age. I share this idea with her. If, in addition, the memories are written down in an entertaining and readable way, as they are in this book, then the result is perfect. Before us, we have a text that conveys the experience of a man who has gone through a long life journey: his childhood in Spain before and during the Civil War, his thirteen years in Cuba as a young man, and his arrival and subsequent life in the United States. There he raised a family, developed his profession as an agricultural engineer specializing in sugarcane, and immersed himself in the American way of life.

Readers will perceive that my dear friend Eugenio (Eugene) Salomon, in writing this memoir, has intensely relived each of the sequences narrated in the chapters of this work. I experienced it myself when I was writing my book about the International Chess Tournaments of Gijón, and he told me that "remembering is reliving a second life." His courage in becoming a writer teaches us that the opportunity to put into words what memory treasures should not be wasted in any way.

Eugene's words convey his thoughts with such veracity that you are taken by the hand and easily become immersed in the events described. You will learn about the origins of his family, his childhood experiences in Gijón during the Spanish Civil War, and his special relationship with his family and friends. You will learn about his beginnings as a competitive chess player and the epiphany of dealing personally with the world champion, Alexander Alekhine, and assimilating his teachings. Of course, you will also understand his courage and ability to overcome difficult moments, such as the consequences for his family of becoming stateless, or of being immersed in the Castro Revolution.

When the co-authors narrate all of the above, there is one aspect that readers will instantly perceive. I am referring to the glow emanating from a passion that permeates the entire book — chess, the game of kings, that has accompanied the protagonist for more than seventy years.

In short, this is a book I have enjoyed very much. It has reaffirmed my conviction that the life events of a human being are always worthy of creating an interesting story to be read with passion. I must thank the co-authors for bringing us, through this magnificent work, all that Eugenio Salomón Rugarcía is. Those who know him already know: This is the story of a wise, good and honest man, a master of chess who, due to the metamorphoses that life provokes, by his own will and for our delight, has known how to play and win on that chessboard that is the life of every person.

Luis Méndez Castedo
Writer and chess historian

CHAPTER 1:
My Parents and their Families

My full name is Juan Eugenio Jose Miguel Manuel Salomon Rugarcía, and every part of that mouthful is part of my identity, part of *me*. Shakespeare asked, "What's in a name?" Actually, quite a lot! In the US, a child typically takes only the father's last name, but in Hispanic culture, a child receives both the father's and mother's last names (paternal, then maternal). Not only does this honor both sides of the child's family, but it also makes it a little easier to trace the family genealogy or to locate your childhood school friends many years later.

My father was Robert Salomon Schwarz, and my mother was Juana Rugarcía Gonzalez-Chavez, so my siblings and I are the Salomon Rugarcía children. I was named **Juan** (for my mother Juana), **Eugenio** (for my godfather, my uncle Eugenio), **Jose** (to honor St. Joseph), **Miguel** (I was born on September 29, the feast day of St. Michael), and chose **Manuel** as my confirmation name. I have been told that there was quite a "discussion" about my name: My mother, Juana, wanted to call me "Juan" after herself, and my uncle/godfather Eugenio wanted me to be named after him. My mother wanted me to be Juan Eugenio, while my godfather wanted Eugenio Juan. It was finally agreed that I was to be baptized Juan Eugenio but that I would be called Eugenio. To this day, I am known professionally as J. Eugene Salomon, although I have always gone by "Eugenio" or "Gene" to family and friends. (I won't even get into the official paperwork nightmare that occurred after 9/11, when the names on all one's documents, including the driver's license, needed to match the passport exactly.)

What makes my story unique, I believe, is that it is more than a little surprising that my parents ever even met, much less married. In those times before widespread public transportation, marriages were typically between people who knew each other from the same or neighboring hometowns. Furthermore, people typically married within their religion and ethnicity. My parents were born on different continents, observed different religions, and were from completely different backgrounds.

Although I have spent the last sixty-plus years of my life in the United States, my roots lie in Spain, Cuba, and Germany, sites of some of the most significant events of the last 130 years of history. We have been through a lot, blessings, tragedies, and adventures; yet through it all, we held together as a family. Thanks to the fortitude and strength of those who came before me, and their fervent belief in the importance of family unity (along with the amazing communication options available today), we are better connected than ever. We are lucky, and we are grateful.

I hope that my readers may enjoy the variety of experiences that I went through, what I like to call "my ninety-four years of coincidences." If Einstein is right in saying that "coincidences are the way of God remaining anonymous," I hope that the message of human solidarity that I learned from my father may help my grandchildren and/or other readers to be less dogmatic and have a kinder heart in their lives.

As I said in the prologue, this book is dedicated to my father, a remarkable man whose strength, resilience, and determination have been my inspiration and guide throughout life. However, to fully understand my life, my motivation, and the pride in my family, it is absolutely necessary to know something about both parents and their lives.

My mother and my Spanish-Cuban roots

My mother's Cuba is a relatively young country. Its ties to Spain began with Columbus' historic trip (financed by Spain) to the "New World" in 1492, and his landing in Cuba on October 28, 1492. He claimed

Chapter 1: My Parents and their Families

the island for the Kingdom of Spain, calling it *"Isla Juana,"* after John, Prince of Asturias, son of Ferdinand and Isabella.

There are varying theories about the origin of the name Cuba, but most attribute the name to words in the original indigenous Taino language: *Cubanacan (kuba-na-kan?)*, meaning "place in the middle" (of the Caribbean), *kuba* (land or terrain), *ciba* (stone, mountain, cave), *cohiba* (tobacco), *cubao* (where fertile land is abundant), and *coabana* (great place).

The first settlement in Cuba was established in the early 1500s, followed by three centuries of Spanish colonization and rule in which sugar and tobacco were established as the island's main products. Cuba's capital city of Havana (*La Habana*, in Spanish), a port conveniently located at the entrance to the Gulf of Mexico, became the main port of Spain's colonies in the Americas. The tropical climate of the island was perfect for growing sugar, and by 1860, it had become Cuba's principal crop. Around this time, Spain lifted strict trade bans, and a great "sugar boom" began.

It was also during this time, the mid-1800s, when my maternal grandfather, Casimiro Rugarcía, left his hometown of Abándames, in the Asturias region of northern Spain. He was barely out of his boyhood, but he went off in search of the Golden Dream like so many emigrants of that time, trying to escape the bleak future that awaited them at home. He decided to emigrate to Cuba (still a Spanish territory at the time), and settled in Cárdenas, about ninety miles from Havana.

In Cuba, Casimiro found work in a grocery store run by another Spaniard. (The store owner, Florencio Fernández del Río, had also come from northern Spain—the town of Ribadesella, only about forty miles from Casimiro's hometown of Abándames.) When Florencio retired, my grandfather took charge of the store, which allowed him to prosper rapidly.

It was in Cárdenas that Casimiro met Juana Gonzalez-Chaves, the daughter of an immigrant from Spain's Canary Islands, and they were married on July 3, 1883. Casimiro and Juana had five children in Cuba: Herminia, Casimiro, Lucrecia, Juanita, and Eugenio—my Cuban roots. Their youngest daughter, my mother, Juana, was born in

1895. (Both my mother and maternal grandmother shared their names with the original name of their beloved island.)

Left: The prologue of my story: my maternal great-grandparents at my grandparents' wedding. **Right**: My grandparents with the five "Cuban roots" (1898); Standing: Aunt Lucrecia (Cachita), Aunt Herminia; Middle row: Uncle Casimiro, my grandmother Juana, my grandfather Casimiro; Bottom row: Uncle Eugenio, my mother, Juana ("Juanita")

In the years before Casimiro's marriage to Juana, the US was in its Reconstruction Era after the Civil War, and Cuba was enjoying a "sugar boom." The country was also trying to gain its independence from Spain, which led to the Cuban War of Independence in 1895. (Not only was that the same year my mother was born, but it was also the year of the death of José Martí—an outstanding poet, a patriot, and a Cuban national hero.)

The War of Cuban Independence, which ultimately led to the Spanish-American War, lasted three years, ending with the Treaty of Paris in 1898. By the terms of the treaty, Spain gave up control of Cuba, and the US obtained Puerto Rico, Guam, and the Philippines. It was simultaneously, I believe, the end of the Spanish Empire and the emergence of the United States as a world power. It was also the first of many significant world conflicts my family would endure.

Chapter 1: My Parents and their Families

Back to Spain

In 1898, after the conflict ended, Abuelito (as I had called my grandfather Casimiro since childhood), decided the moment had come for him and his family, the Rugarcías, to return to Spain. (I guess he felt more like a Spaniard than an independent Cuban.) Together with his family, Abuelito boarded the ship *Alfonso XIII*, and set sail for Santander, on the northern coast of Spain, hoping to return to his beloved Abándames. Fortunately, he had done well financially in Cuba, and was able to return to Spain a rich man. Many years of long days of work had made him an *"indiano,"* the generic name used in Spain to designate the emigrants who had gone to "the Americas" and returned to Spain as rich men.

Abuelito did not settle his family in his hometown of Abándames, but decided instead to relocate in Gijón, where, years later (1912), he would buy the famous *"Villa Gil,"* changing the name to *"Villa Almendares"* after the Almendares River in Havana. It became the Rugarcía family's summer resort for almost thirty years, providing the most wonderful memories for the eight cousins of the Menendez Rugarcía and Salomon Rugarcía families—memories I treasure to this day. That was how my aunts Herminia and Lucrecia (Cachita), my uncles Casimiro and Eugenio, and my mother (Juanita) came to be in Gijón (Asturias region) just at the very end of the nineteenth century.

My mother Juanita

My mother and her siblings were fortunate enough to enjoy a privileged life because my grandfather had been financially successful in Cuba. All five children were able to have private music lessons as well as oil painting lessons, which enriched their lives forever.

My mother, Juanita, is our unsung family heroine. In the chapters that follow, you will read how she was our rock, raising her children in terribly difficult times, and supporting her husband through all manner of adversity, but there is more to her and her family than just that. I have very dear memories of her cooking *platanos fritos*, a traditional Cuban delicacy. (She was very fond of them, and I loved them, too!)

Obviously, my mother learned to cook from her mother, who was born and raised in Cuba, and she made absolutely delicious black beans and rice (a typical Cuban dish) for us while we were growing up in Spain.

In her younger years, my mother had been a concert-quality pianist. Later in life, even when she had her hands full performing the roles of father and mother, she would still find time to play some of my favorite music at the piano.

Some of the early memories of my mother are of playing *tresillo* (a little-known card game) with her, my grandfather, and my aunt "Cachita" (Lucrecia), in Gijón, Spain, right after the Spanish Civil War years. Years later, in Cuba, I also remember playing canasta with her and my sister-in-law, Chicha. (I have no doubt these experiences contributed to my current love of bridge!)

(In writing these stories, I almost laugh out loud remembering with love that for years, even as a teenage boy, I thought that the "bidet" in our bathroom was just a comfortable place to wash your feet…as my mother used to do when I was a child!!)

Juanita's siblings

My aunt Herminia was several years older than her siblings, and she married quite young, which resulted in our four Menendez Rugarcía cousins being much older than us, the four Salomon Rugarcías. Herminia's husband, my "tío Luis" (Luis Menendez de Juan), was an industrialist from Gijón.

My aunt Lucrecia ("Cachita") was married late in life to a widower from Catalonia with a teenage daughter—our step cousin, Carmela Villaret—with whom we stayed connected over the years. Carmela married Manuel Puertas, the founder of Euro-Building, a famous hotel of apartments, which was a very new concept in Spain at that time. (I visited with Manuel on one of my vacations in Spain, sometime in the late '70s or '80s, and he offered me the opportunity to become his agent for the sale of his hotel condominiums in the US. Since I was still in love with my career in the sugar and food ingredients business, I didn't take him up on his offer. I may have missed a chance to become a rich man…but who knows? My life has been rich in many other ways.

My uncle Casimiro did not have any children. He went on to become a doctor and was the personal physician of World Chess Champion Alexander Alekhine, whose advice to me would later be significant in my life. Later in life, "*Tío Casi*" (Uncle Casi) published a book of poetry titled: *Páginas de mi diario* (*Pages from my Diary*). The book was reviewed in 1971 by my friend, the great journalist and chess master, Pablo Morán. Pablo wrote, "Dr. Casimiro Rugarcía, Gijón doctor and extraordinary poet, has just published a book of exceptional quality. In the pages of his book there is life and heart and soul." I still proudly keep his book on my night table, the leather-bound copy he dedicated to Bea and me during our visit in Madrid in 1971. A few months later, Pablo Morán dedicated his chess column in Gijón's newspaper "*Voluntad*" to "Dr. Casimiro Rugarcía, Poet and Chess Player." In the article, Pablo printed a never-before-published poem about chess written by my Uncle Casi, a true poet of chess. (I had the privilege of learning the poetic way of playing chess from him!!) I can proudly assure my readers that this poem by "Tío Casi" is the best ever written about chess:

"Es el ajedrez sin par, Imagen fiel de la vida,
Desesperada partida contra el tiempo y el azar;
Partida donde suele hallar nuestro débil corazón,
Además de humillación, una amargura tan fiera
Como si al perder muriera su mas hermosa ilusión…."

"Chess is without peer, a true image of life,
A desperate game against time and chance
A battle where our weak hearts sometimes find
not just humiliation, but a bitterness so fierce at losing,
as if one's most beautiful dreams were dying…"

My uncle Eugenio, my godfather, the one who eventually introduced my father to my mother, was a truly brilliant man. As a student, he was reportedly the best ever on record at the high school level in

Gijón. Later in life, he was, at different times, the dean of the Madrid University School of Industrial Engineers, the *"Consejero Delegado"* (president) of the Italian-Spanish company SNIACE (*Sociedad Nacional Industrias Aplicación Celulosa Española*), and the *"Director General de Industrias"* of the Spanish government under Franco.

My Uncle Eugenio (kissing the hand of Queen Sofia) as he receives a visit from King Juan Carlos and Queen Sofia to the SNIACE factory in Torrelavega, Northern Spain.

Uncle Eugenio had only one child, my cousin Miguel Rugarcía (seven years my junior). Cousin Miguel was an official medical doctor to the Spanish Senate. He had two daughters, Myriam and Covadonga, and one son, Luis, who lives in Seville. Luis is, in effect, the end of the Casimiro Rugarcía dynasty since he has three daughters but no sons. My grandchildren are still in contact with his daughters. In 2017, we enjoyed a beautiful vacation together with our granddaughter, Nina, in Seville, staying at Luis Rugarcía's small *"cortijo"* (deluxe countryside place). Nina's sister, Ella, has also met Luis' daughters, and my son Robbie's family has also been in contact with them since their initial meeting several years ago.

It is with a smile of satisfaction that when I write all the details of this long story, I feel truly proud of having kept these relationships alive so that the great-great grandchildren of my *abuelito* are still in touch. This is the origin of the well-known Rugarcía family from Gijón—my Spanish and Cuban roots.

Chapter 1: My Parents and their Families

The importance of education

Upon reflection about my Rugarcía side, it is amazing to me how many of them became medical doctors or educators. The family's focus on the importance of advanced education continued for generations. In addition to my Uncle Casimiro's medical profession, my brother Roberto, first cousin Miguel Rugarcía, two of my brother Roberto's children (Maria Cristina Salomon and Roberto Salomon), and two of my sister Mela's children (Tony Moriyon and Maria Carmen Moriyon) all went on to become doctors. My first cousin, Luis Menendez Rugarcía, became both a medical doctor and a dentist.

The family also has had an extraordinary number of educators. My uncle Eugenio was the dean and a professor at Madrid University School of Industrial Engineers, my cousin Luchy taught high school physics, and my sister Ana Maria briefly taught German at my high school (Jovellanos Institute in Gijón) and later taught Spanish in England and Jamaica. My nephew, Roberto Moriyon, was a professor at Madrid University; my son, Robert Salomon, is a professor at New York University; my daughter Maria is an elementary school teacher in New Jersey; and our son Henry taught math in Texas for several years. I myself was a first-grade teacher at the Belén Jesuit school in Havana from 1948–1949, and then taught at the Havana University School of Agricultural and Sugar Chemistry Engineering ten years later.

Finally, Abuelito's first three granddaughters ("Chuqui," "Luchy," and "Tete") were all university graduates and educators who founded the "Academia Rugarcía," a prestigious women's academy in Gijón. It is important to remember that in the 1920s and 1930s, in Spain as well as in the United States, it was very uncommon for young women to attend universities, get degrees, and pursue careers—but my three cousins did just that! I remember them with love and admiration to this day, as outstanding examples of the Rugarcía family's dedication to education.

My father and my German roots

On my father's side, we are fortunate enough to have a wealth of genealogical information.

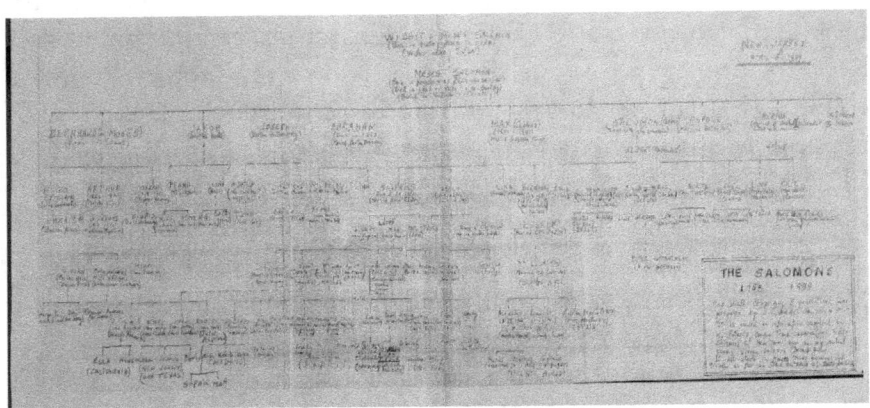

Family tree, developed from the original documents from my father's first cousin, Frank Sanders (born Frank Salomon in Germany). Three of my father's cousins, children of his Uncle Leopold were victims of the Nazi genocide.

As you can see, the above genealogical tree: "The Salomons 1758–1999" comprises eight generations and was prepared by me based on the information supplied by my father's cousin Frank Sanders of New York, and by my distant cousin, Vivian Salomon (Buenos Aires).

I did not research it, and it may contain errors or omissions. I leave it up to the grandchildren or great-grandchildren of the Salomon-Schwarz family to complete and further research. I will leave all the original information, including the Last Will and Testament of Moses Salomon (1795–1867), written in German and Hebrew, with my children.

Chapter 1: My Parents and their Families

The Salomons—1758 and onward

It all starts in 1758, in Mutzig, Alsace (France-Germany), and travels as far as Spain, Australia, the US, South America…and the rest of the world.

At the very top of my father's side of the family tree, Wibbit or Moses Salomon was born in 1758 in the town of Mutzig, in the Alsace region of (what was then) France. His wife's name was Esther, and they were Jewish. Wibbit was born right in the middle of the Seven Years' War in Europe, and since then, the Salomon family history has been substantially affected by European and global conflicts.

Alsace was one of the largest Jewish settlement areas in the territory of present-day France, but it was not easy being Jewish in Alsace. Having been expelled from the region's major cities, Jews were permitted to settle in the villages nearby but were required to be counted for the "General Enumeration of the Jews Tolerated in the Province of Alsace." In 1689, there were 522 Jewish families living in the entire Alsace region, but by 1740, that number had grown to 2,125. (Mutzig was one of the Jewish communities named in the Enumeration of 1784, noting that 307 Jewish persons lived there.). As non-citizens, Jews were subjected to additional restrictions and taxes. It was not until 1791, during the French Revolution, that they became citizens with the same rights and responsibilities.[1]

As if that wasn't difficult enough, Alsace has changed hands between France and Germany several times during the last two centuries of my family's history in the region. When Wibbit was born in 1758, Alsace belonged to France—and the US did not yet exist as an independent nation.

Wibbit's son, Moses Salomon, was born in 1795 in Hochheim am

---
1 https://www.jewishgen.org/french/kallmann.htm

Rhein. He and his wife, Lina Danzig, had nine children (see picture). Among them was my great-grandfather Max (in the top hat) who was born in 1821 in Coblenz. Max married Johanna Folda, and they had seven children, including my grandfather, Siegfried, born in 1854. Siegfried married Anna Sarah Schwarz, and they had three sons, Paul, Max, and Robert—my father.

My father, Robert

My father, Robert Israel Salomon, was born on September 19, 1895. Robert and his brothers, Paul and Max, were born and raised in Metz, (about ninety-five miles from Mutzig) in the historical Alsace-Lorraine region that has belonged to both France and Germany at different points in history. At that time, Metz (and the entire Alsace-Lorraine region) had just become German territory via the Treaty of Frankfurt in 1871, at the end of the Franco-Prussian War. The citizens of Metz were given until October 1872 to decide whether to retain French citizenship and leave the area or to stay and become German citizens. The family decided to stay and received full German citizenship.

When you come into this world, nobody asks you to which community or race you would like to belong to or which religion you prefer to follow. My paternal grandparents, Siegfried Salomon and Anna Schwarz, were Jewish. They wanted to share with their children their love for life, maximum tolerance, respect for freedom and human diversity, and appreciation for all that was good and beautiful in the world. In Jewish families, it was customary for young people to travel outside their native country gathering experiences and learning languages…which my father did. Shortly before the outbreak of World War I, he became an apprentice in the Gijón, Spain, office of German company AEG and spent part of his youth enjoying the beautiful landscapes (and cider!) of the region of Asturias, in northern Spain.

He got the management trainee position just weeks before World War I began, and his brothers, Paul and Max, were soon fighting WWI for Germany. His mother, my *Grossmama*, distressed at already having two sons fighting at the front for the German army, was afraid that my father, who always did his duty, would also want to return to Germany

Chapter 1: My Parents and their Families

to fight in the war for his country. She decided to write to the German consul in Gijón, Spain, to ask, after explaining the situation with her other two sons, that they not grant his visa to return to Germany. The consul showed understanding and compassion, and granted her request, blocking my father from leaving Spain.

Left: My grandparents, Anna Schwarz and Sigfrid Salomon with their three sons. **Right**: Their home in Metz, Germany.

Alone in a strange country and separated from his family, my father, Robert, lived in the small house of a farming family on the outskirts of Gijón. He was an avid and expert cello player and found refuge in classical music, swimming, and trips to the famous *Picos de Europa* mountains. One of the people who would occasionally also be on the trips was Eugenio Rugarcía, my mother's brother, and the two men discovered they shared a love of music.

It was through that shared love of music that my parents met. Around 1917, Juanita's brother (my uncle) Eugenio invited Robert Salomon, with whom he had enjoyed excursions into the Picos de Europa mountains, to play in a quartet at the Rugarcía house, where my mother Juana was the pianist. Three years later, Robert and Juana were married, and my sister Ana Maria was born the following year in Gijón. Two years after that, my father got his first promotion, and the family moved from Gijón to the beautiful city of Valencia (on the Mediterranean coast), where my brother Roberto was born. My father enjoyed rapid success in his management career, and within a few years, he was transferred to the AEG main office in Madrid as an executive.

Although the family now lived in Madrid, Robert and Juana's next two children, my sister Mela (Maria del Carmen) and myself, were born in Gijón, surrounded by all the love and support of my mother's great family, the Rugarcías. We typically spent our summers with them in Gijón, and since Mela's birthday was during the summer, and my birthday is in September, it made more sense for my mother to remain in Gijón rather than to undertake the ten-hour train ride to Madrid while eight months pregnant.

Yes, paths can cross and even unite, even if their starting points are complete opposites, as Robert's and Juana's origins were. My mother's family was Catholic and conservative-minded, while my father came from a different background: Jewish and liberal thinkers. But love always finds a way and is capable of surmounting even the highest barriers.

In addition to the remarkably unlikely meeting of my parents, my father experienced many noteworthy incidents during his life and kept detailed journals of his life in Europe during WWI, the Spanish Civil War, and WWII. Years ago, our niece Ani (now Spain's ambassador to Israel), undertook the arduous task of turning the memoirs of her grandfather (originally written in Spanish and German) into a book in Spanish: *Caminar y Cavilar: Cuentos bajo el signo de la Cruz y a la sombra de la cruz gamada* (*Walking and Wondering: Living under the Sign of the Cross in the Shadow of the Swastika*). Several years ago, my son Henry and I completed our labor of love and translated that book into English (available as an e-book). The following comments are taken from Henry's notes:

> *"The English version took countless hours, reams of paper, and lots of research. Written Spanish is much different from written English.... Further, the register and tone were much more formal. Getting the literal translation and, more importantly, the meaning of not only what my grandfather said but what he meant, required reading and re-reading the Spanish text and figuring out context. I spent countless hours on the phone with my father and even more time on the internet*

researching dates, facts, and historical events to make sure the information presented was as historically accurate as possible. My hope is that you enjoy my grandfather's adventures as much as I did. Certain stories are not meant to disappear in history. I believe this is one of them."

During his life (1895–1968), my father was an eyewitness to the First World War, the Spanish Civil War, the Second World War, and the Cuban Revolution. After reading his book, one would think that he was an adventurer, but in reality, he was an idealist striving to conduct a productive, "normal" life. Whether in high-management positions at AEG in Spain, as an owner of his own store, as a cellist in the Havana Philharmonic Orchestra, selling watches throughout Cuba, or later, acting as an executive for an American company in Madrid, he always believed in the virtue of hard work.

He was a converted (and devout) Catholic, and his idols were Gandhi and Don Quixote. His favorite sports were mountain excursions (he knew the Picos de Europa mountain range like few people did) and swimming (for years, he was the best long-distance swimmer in Asturias). Not only did he have a passion for classical music, but as an avid reader (in Spanish, French, and German), his knowledge of philosophy, history, and literature was truly impressive.

My Onkel Paul

Paul Salomon was the oldest of the brothers. Born June 1, 1886, Paul was almost ten years older than Robert and Max, who were close in age. He had two children, Lothar and Heidi. In the early 1930s (I guess, 1932), while Grossmama was living with us in Spain, he and his son Lothar came to visit us in Madrid. That was the only time in my life that I saw Uncle Paul and Cousin Lothar. Obviously, I do not remember them since I was only about three years old at the time.

Back row: Uncle Paul, Grossmama, my father, Robert, and Lothar.
Front row: My brother Robert, my sister Mela, German "Juanchu" (Uncle Max's son), and a neighbor

As Hitler came to power and the Jewish persecution began, Uncle Paul found a way to save his two youngsters—by sending them to Australia with some friends. Over the years, my sister Ana Maria (the "ambassador" of the family) always stayed connected with the family around the world and kept in close touch with Lothar.

A few years back, I had the joy of meeting one of Lothar's sons (Paul's grandson), Dr. Ralph Salmon from the UK, during a vacation in which we were both in Madrid. Ralph is a close friend of my niece "Nenuca" (my sister Mela's daughter Maria Carmen, who is also a medical doctor). They had met with the help of my sister Ana Maria.

When I decided to convert this book from a chess-oriented book to a family-oriented one, I called Ralph in London (or so I thought) using that marvelous tool called WhatsApp, and he answered his cell phone…from Australia, where he was visiting his mother. Following are a couple of his family pictures that he sent to me:

Left: Paul Salomon, October 1945; **Center:** Lothar and Dora Salmon, May 1946, Australia; **Right:** Lothar and Dora, with their sons Ralph and Grant

Chapter 1: My Parents and their Families

Uncle "Onkel" Max

My father, Robert, the youngest of the three brothers, was not the only one of his siblings to have experienced and survived significant hardships. The middle brother, my Onkel Max (born March 7, 1894), endured a life similar to my father's—intense and full of the kinds of events that happen in times of war. His story, which is also full of suffering and heroism, ends with exile.

As my father related it to me, Max fought for the German army during World War I. (Robert was working in Spain.) Things became difficult when he was gravely wounded in the Battle of the Argonne Forest and had to be transferred to a hospital in Freiburg, in the Black Forest region. During Max's stay in the hospital, he was kept in isolation because some suspicions of espionage had arisen about him. These suspicions had their roots in the letters my father had written to his brother from Spain when he found out about Max's situation. The military censor had questioned what was in these letters from so far away, and that was reason enough for a dangerous suspicion of espionage to appear.

When Max recovered from his wounds, due to the general unease surrounding him from the espionage suspicions, he was sent to the Russian front. Within a few weeks, he was taken prisoner and was taken to Jansk, Siberia, where he had to fight to survive the severe conditions. Plague, cholera, and typhus ran rampant in the prison camp, but my uncle Max managed to survive everything and was counted among the few captives (out of two thousand) who survived. Luck was truly at his side, however. He fell ill with typhus, and in his suffering, he would curse in French ("*Sacre Coeur!*"). One of the medics (who was French) was surprised that a German spoke French so fluently and began speaking with my uncle. When he found out that Uncle Max was from Metz, the French doctor interceded with his superiors and succeeded in having my uncle Max returned to Moscow, on his way to Metz. Miraculously, Max survived the trip in an open sled, in full winter, with temperatures of -30 C and a fever that reached 40 C. He finally reached Moscow but was in bad shape—more out of this world than in it.

Sweet Memories — Family, Friends, Chess, and Sugar

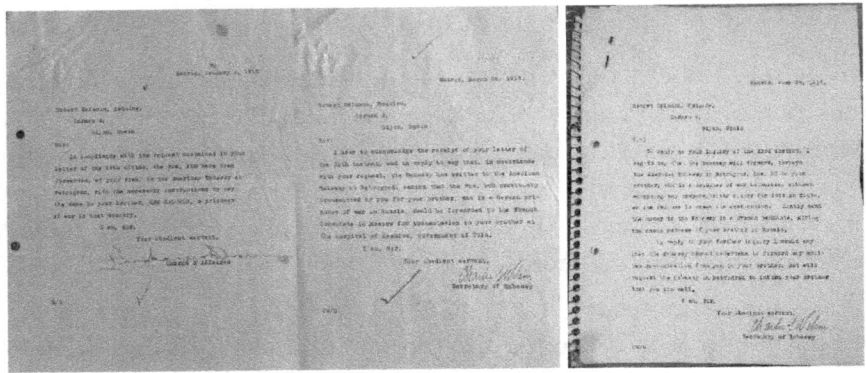

Correspondence between my father and the US Embassy in Madrid, regarding my father's inquiries and money sent to his brother (1916).

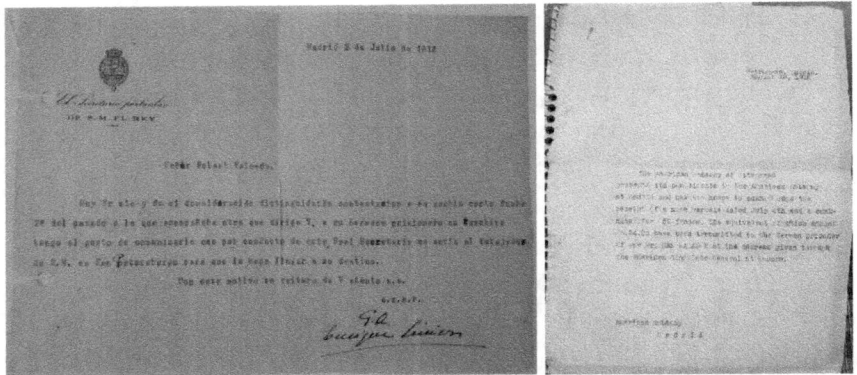

Left: Letter from the secretary of the King of Spain regarding my father's attempt to send money to his brother, Max. **Right**: Finally—a response from Russia.

My uncle Max remained there for a long while, recovering from everything, but something changed inside him during his time in Russia, affecting the vision he had of the world. The things he saw and heard there may have influenced his political views, making him an extreme leftist.

Just before my parents' wedding in 1920, Uncle Max visited Spain. He loved the country and decided to leave everything behind to settle there, thanks partly to my father's contacts through his management position at the German AEG company. He later moved to Madrid and opened his own business, House of Max Salomon (a store that sold replacement bicycle parts), which, over time, prospered and grew. He married Maria Concepcion "Concha" Cazalis (sister of well-known jai-alai players Ricardo and Segundo Cazalis) and eventually moved to the Dominican Republic and then Mexico. They had two sons, my first cousins Ernesto and German "Juanchu").

Left and middle: Max Salomon and Concepcion (Concha) Cazalis, visa photos, 1945. **Right:** Max Salomon, painting that now hangs in the house of one of his granddaughters.

A special connection to my father

I have always felt especially connected to my father—the influence of his life, and perhaps of his spirit, in my long life is truly curious. Things have happened to me where dreams, memories, coincidences, and mysteries have been acutely present. I have always considered myself a man of science, so I look for a rational explanation for everything that happens around me. Nevertheless, I must admit that sometimes unknown and disconcerting things happen that the mind cannot comprehend... but my heart reminds me that I *did* feel and experienced them!

I share this curious trait with my father (who also went through situations that were impossible to explain), which he addressed in his memoir, *Walking and Wondering: Living under the Sign of the Cross in the Shadow of the Swastika*, where he writes: "Many people do not believe in mental telepathy, but I have not the slightest doubt of its existence, even if science has not yet discovered what kind of waves it uses, or how they are received." Here is just one example.

> *"When my brother Max was seriously injured in 1915 and transferred to a clinic in Freiburg, I had a dream: I saw him with two other soldiers, also wearing German uniforms, defending a trench against a band of Russian Cossacks charging with bayonets... I began to ponder... Nothing could have happened since I knew that my brother was in a hospital* [in Freiburg, far from Russia]."

My father knew that Max had been wounded at the French front, so it did not make sense that he would be fighting Russians. Because the dream was so curious, Robert wrote down the date. However, what my father did not know was that Max had been released from the hospital and sent to the Russian front. A few years later, when Max visited the family in Spain, my father asked Max about the incident—it had happened exactly as in the dream...on the very same day that Robert dreamed it.

In 1916, my father had another dream—this one about walking through a beautiful, familiar-feeling landscape, but he was completely at a loss as to where he must have seen it. Five weeks later, he received a letter in Max's handwriting, postmarked from France. In the letter, Max described having walked through an area that was remarkably similar to the area in the Lorraine Valley where they had grown up. Coincidence? I suppose it is possible, but as my father noted in his memoirs,

> *"...Full of surprise at these incomprehensible things, and after several times reading the letter that was 'dreamed before received,' I recalled a verse by the great Shakespeare: 'There are more things in heaven and earth, Horatio, than are dreamt of in your philosophy.'"*

These experiences are not limited to just this anecdote. For reasons that I do not understand, while I sleep, my brain continues working. As a psychologist once explained to me, it is nothing to worry about, nor is it unique.

With my wife, Beatrice, as a witness, I frequently wake at all hours of the night with the solution to a problem that has been insistently

Chapter 1: My Parents and their Families

rolling around in my head, ranging from a move that I should have made in some chess game to how to approach a business situation or article. Is it possible that one's dreams, memories, and spirit are connected in some way that the human mind cannot comprehend? Matter and energy transform into each other; time and space behave as if they are the same. Time passes and the universe expands…and my curious mind wonders: What happens to your memories? Do they become part of your spirit and live on, or are they lost forever? Hopefully, this recording of some of my memories will keep them from being lost forever.

CHAPTER 2:
Family Life and War through the Eyes of a Child
(1921–1943)

We were the four Salomon Rugarcía siblings. My sister Ana Maria, born in Gijón, in 1921, was the oldest of the four of us and was seven years my senior. She was not my playmate because of the difference in our ages, but she was always a clear leader with a very clear mind. For her one-hundredth birthday, we had big plans to have our last vacation in Spain to celebrate her "one century" of extraordinary life…but the COVID pandemic made it impossible. Instead, we created a book for her, containing beautiful messages, photos, and memories of the love that surrounds her in our family.

My mother with my three siblings, circa 1927. I had either not been born yet or was too young for photographs.

Sweet Memories — Family, Friends, Chess, and Sugar

Ana Maria celebrated turning 101 years old this past December in Madrid. (Some of the messages appear in a later chapter.)

My father had gotten a promotion, and the family moved from Gijón to Valencia—from a beautiful Atlantic Ocean beach to the warmer climate beaches of the Mediterranean. My brother Roberto was born in Valencia, Spain in 1922. Six years my senior, Roberto was not my playmate either but was a model that I looked up to, to imitate. He was always very smart and very happy and never gave my parents any trouble. I guess that I always looked at him with a mixture of admiration and perhaps a bit of envy. Shortly before his fortieth birthday, with three little children (ages seven, five, and six months) and a brilliant career in front of him, cancer took him away from us. There are sad episodes that remain engraved in your memory forever. The untimely death of my older brother Robert is one of the most tragic of my memories, sixty years ago.

The younger sister, Maria del Carmen, "Mela," was born in Gijón, in 1924. Mela was only four years older than me, so I interacted and played with her more than I did with the older ones. I remember one time, when I was maybe five years old, when we were having a barbecue, and we had long branches of small trees on fire. I got the great idea of trying to hit her with the red, burning tip of a branch. (I am ashamed to say that I was delighted to scare her.) We ran all over the garden until I caught her and gave her a lifelong scar on her upper arm. (Sorry, Mela...) She was the only one of the siblings who never came to Cuba—she married in 1948 and remained in Spain. I can say, however, that she was always the heart and the center of our family union. She died in Madrid at age ninety-three. When Mela's final days arrived, I decided to take a week's vacation and spend it with her while she was still lucid. What was also emotional for me was that two of my sons and one granddaughter decided to come along, a clear return of all the love she had conveyed to them in their childhood. I believe that the week we spent together for a final family farewell is the best illustration of the family union that I so much cherish and try to leave for my grandchildren as an example to follow.

Growing up, we each had a nickname—Ana Maria was "Cuca" (Where did it come from? No idea), Roberto was "Tito" (the short form of Robertito), Maria del Carmen was "Mela" (from Carmela), and I was Eugenín (for "Little Eugenio" since I was the youngest). My parents, siblings, and cousins—the family—used the nicknames; however, in Mela's case, it was more broadly used.

German children in Spain

My father had always felt immensely proud of his German heritage and of not having changed nationality/citizenship when Alsace Lorraine (where he was born) became part of France after World War I. Because of this, he proudly registered the four of us at the German consulate right at birth. Despite being born in Spain, the four of us were German citizens, and even my mother acquired German citizenship.

Although we lived in Madrid, we spent the summers at Abuelito's estate in Gijón. Prior to 1932, we were all enrolled in the Deutsche Spanish school in Madrid, but I only attended kindergarten there. Since my brother and sisters had gone to German school for several years, all three of them were fluent in German. In 1932 or 1933, my father was becoming increasingly uncomfortable with the antisemitic atmosphere at AEG, so he left the company, took us all out of the German school, and put us in the "Instituto Escuela" in Madrid—a very prestigious academy. (Seventy years later, my son Robbie took a sabbatical year from NYU and decided to take his family to Madrid for a year so his children could be bilingual. He enrolled them in the very prestigious school that was the successor to the school we attended as children.)

My father had a good job so we could afford a comfortable life. He had an automobile and a chauffeur, which was not very common in those days. Almost all of us took music lessons—my brother, like my father, played the cello; Ana Maria played the violin; and Mela, like my mother, played the piano. (I never got the chance to have music lessons because the war started.)

Summers at Abuelito's

Every summer, the eight cousins of the Menéndez Rugarcía and Salomon Rugarcía families would get together at Abuelito's *finca* (country estate) in Mareo, outside of Gijón. Those were times of innocence, happiness, and games—we were blissfully ignorant of what the future would bring. The four Menendez Rugarcía cousins: three girls (Maria Herminia "Chuqui," Maria Luisa "Luchy," and Maria Teresa "Tete") and a boy, Luis, were Aunt Herminia and Uncle Luis' children and were many years older than me.

My grandparents, parents, and cousins (circa 1922) at Villa Almendares (Abuelito's estate), taken well before I was born.

The estate, *Villa Almendares*, was located 5 km from Gijón and was a lovely, pleasant place. It was next to the "*finca*" (summer estate) owned by "los del San Luis," the family that owned the well-known San Luis clothing store in Gijón. I remember them well: Pepita, Colito, and Marujina became friends for life, beginning with our shared love of Mareo in the 1930s and continuing with our bicycle excursions to the Estaño Beach in the early '40s. On the other side of Abuelito's *finca* was the summer estate of the Balbona family, but I do not remember having met any of them in childhood. However, a dozen years later in Havana, in one of the many coincidences of my life, I became friendly with one member of the Balbona family who was my age while we were both members of the *Agrupación Católica Universitaria* in Cuba.

At Villa Almendares, there was a silo for grain storage, a stable with twenty Holstein cows, a small cider-bottling plant for the apples from the farm's own orchard, a henhouse, a small patch of woods, and the manor house (in front of which I organized many snail races). It was a paradise for children whose only thoughts were about play. I was probably around five years old when my cousin Luis taught me how to capture beetles so they wouldn't bite and how to tell if a beetle was male or female. (The males bite.) He also taught me to recognize the constellations in the night sky.

I remember that we once had a little dog that would run after us in the garden. I was aggravated because the older kids never paid attention to me. One day, the dog jumped on me (nothing serious), but I went and told Abuelito that the dog had bitten me, and he got rid of the dog. I felt terrible, and I am sure my siblings and my cousins were not happy with me.

It was also there that I made, and lost, my first childhood friend—Alvarín, the son of the estate's caretakers, Nieves and Arturo. On the rare sunny mornings in Asturias, Alvarín and I searched the garden and the apple orchard for snails to race. We drew a starting and a finish line on the road that ran in front of the house, and with the help of a toothpick, we raced our snails to victory.

In the summer of 1935, when I wasn't yet seven years old, I suggested to Alvarín that instead of collecting snails every day for that day's competition, it would be more efficient to collect a bucket of them, which would supply us for a while. (I suppose that was the first hint of the planning mind usually associated with a chess master or a management consultant—my future activities where problem-solving skills are extremely important.) Maintaining our valuable inventory was easy—I put the small pail of snails under my bed. Unfortunately, a few hours later, when my mother came into my room to make the bed, she was horrified to find quite a colorful collection of snails climbing up the walls. That was undoubtedly the end of our snail races, but that childhood memory will be with me forever.

As I write about these first childhood memories, another anecdote about Alvarín has come to mind. One day, some visitors came to Villa Almendares (I do not remember who they were, or why they were there). They stood admiring the beauty of the estate and asked us,

"Who are the owners?" I responded with pride, "Abuelito!" By some miracle of the human mind, I still remember the gentle correction in Alvarín's answer, "Eugenín, my father also owns a small part, because he works for it." I suppose that was my first lesson in socialism.

Several years later, during the Spanish Civil War, the Republicans took the estate to use as an artillery headquarters. Tragically, Alvarín found a grenade somewhere in the grass, and it exploded in his hands. When I found out, upon my family's return to Gijón after having been evacuated to France, I cried over my first friend who was so unfairly lost!

Meanwhile, my father had been promoted to an executive position in the main office of his company in Madrid. The family (now complete), lived there until 1936, the beginning of the Spanish Civil War. Up to this moment, you could say that for all practical purposes, I did not know my father. I had just vague recollections of life at four to seven years of age in Madrid, the years before the war when he was with us, but a few memories still remain. I remember the classical music quartets on weekends with my mother at the piano and my father at his cello. I also remember Grossmama with her odd accent, and the German Christmas songs my mother played on the piano while my sisters, brother, father, and I sang.

I also remember one other incident involving Grossmama. In those days, there were no pens, just inkwells, and I had started to play with the ink container from my father's desk. It fell onto the Persian rug, and Grossmama sternly said to me, "Wait til your father comes home!" I was so scared! I stayed by the door until my father arrived and quickly begged him, "Papa—don't talk to Grossmama. She's going to tell you that I spilled the ink on the rug!"

I guess these were the happy times and stories of an affluent family—we had no idea how fortunate we were. It is astounding how everything can change from absolute calm to disaster in a matter of days—the blink of an eye. An innocent child, protected by his family, blessedly has no idea what is happening around him. Sadly, that illusion cannot endure forever, and sooner or later, reality hits hard.

Chapter 2: Family Life and War through the Eyes of a Child

The Spanish Civil War begins—July 18, 1936

Those carefree times were left behind much too soon due to the start of the Spanish Civil War in the summer of 1936. What started as conservatives versus liberals soon would end with the radical right (fascists) versus radical left (communists). The winds of war blew hard, destroying everything we knew and tossing my family and our possessions in all directions. My Salomon cousins and I were robbed of our childhood and separated for quite some time, scattered across the world seemingly without rhyme or reason. Wars, where everyone loses and so many lives are affected, had a significant impact on my family. The world was being torn into two irreconcilable parts, and Spain was a prime example of this radical division. This led to a disastrous civil war, and my family was one of many fractured by the eruption of the conflict in 1936.

That July, my parents had remained in Madrid while we spent the summer in Gijón, at my grandparents' house as we usually did. The conflict prevented us from reuniting as a family later that summer and for several years thereafter.

There is an amazing story about my father's friendship with a famous Spanish general, General Jose Miaja, the Defender of Madrid. When my father was a youngster, recently arrived in Asturias from Germany, he and the general became friends through their shared frequent excursions to the Picos de Europa mountains. (They were such close friends that my sister used to call Miaja "Tio Pepe.") Miaja was then a colonel in the Spanish army and was stationed in Oviedo. The interaction between my father and General Miaja during the Spanish Civil War in Madrid resulted in saving lives and is well-described in my father's memoirs.

We would soon learn first-hand the harshness of war. I remember going to sleep in my room on July 18, enjoying the view of my beloved Begoña Park, and waking the next morning on the floor in the total darkness of a windowless room. The Siege of Gijón (July 19 to August 16, 1936), one of the early battles in the Spanish Civil War, had begun. While I slept, my family had moved my siblings and me to another room to protect us. Our house, San Bernardo 135 (today's number 81), was not far from the besieged *"Cuartel de Simancas"* whose garrison was loyal to Franco but was surrounded by "republican forces". The shootings were happening all over town. Soon, the ship *Almirante Cervera* would arrive in Gijón, and would start firing on the troops surrounding the Simancas fortress—the shells were flying directly over our building! We (the four Salomon Rugarcía children, ages seven to fourteen) had just been enjoying the summer near the beach, waiting for our parents who were still at home in Madrid, when our lives were changed forever.

As the fighting raged on, I distinctly remember one day walking with my older sister (Ana Maria, now one hundred years old and living in Majadahonda, Madrid) when a German Stuka plane flew over us, machine-gunning the open street, the *Paseo de Begoña*. I will never forget my sister Ani pulling me by the arm and us running like hell to safety through the first open door we found.

I can also remember the hunger and the deprivation, the days when we could only trick our stomachs into feeling full by eating *algarrobas* (carob beans). They were sold through the government-controlled stores, and you could only get them if you were lucky. I also desperately missed my grandparents' farm estate and being able to play in the park—small concerns for adults, perhaps, but I was just a seven- or eight-year-old boy, and they felt like true hardships to me. There we all were, us four children, my three older female cousins, and my grandfather and "Cachita" (my widowed Aunt Lucrecia) in the spacious duplex apartment at San Bernardo 135 overlooking Gijón's beautiful Begoña Park but unable to go out to play because it was much too dangerous!

With my parents stuck in Madrid and us in Gijón, my three female cousins (Chuqui, Luchy, and Teté, already young adults), tried to be the mother I had temporarily lost due to separation by the war. Their brother, my dear cousin Luis, was not with us. (By the time war came, he was a student at a university and was recruited by Franco.) I will never forget my cousin Luchy (María Luisa) reciting this traditional poem (Espronceda's *"Cancion del Pirata"*) as I sat on her lap:

Chapter 2: Family Life and War through the Eyes of a Child

*"Ten cannons on each side, an aft wind filling the sails,
not crossing the sea but flying, came a brigantine sailboat…"*

Hypnotized by her delivery, I asked who had written such a beautiful poem, and she responded, "I did!" With that, Luchy had won my eternal admiration. (Those three cousins were well-known in Gijón for being owners and teachers in the family-run academy, *Academia Menéndez Rugarcía*.)

Group picture of the Menéndez Rugarcía Academy (1935) with my three cousins. **Standing, from left:** María Luisa ("Luchy," fourth), Maria Teresa ("Tete," fifth), María Herminia ("Chuqui," eighth)

In mid-1937, we were all evacuated from Gijón (including my uncle, grandfather, and cousins), aboard the *USS Kane I*, an American destroyer sent to rescue all US and Latin American citizens from the war zone in northern Spain. (Thanks to my mother's Cuban heritage, we were able to be included.) All the children slept on the deck of the ship, and I remember a tall officer who gave chocolate bars to us, the youngest children—an incredible treat after so many months of hunger! After spending a few days in the French town of St. Jean de Luz, and a few weeks in Zamora (a town in Spain, already under Franco's control), we were able to return to Gijón, where the situation had calmed down, but everything had changed. The streets were empty, and you could still hear occasional gunshots ("*los pacos*").

In late 1937, knowing that we children were safe with Abuelito in Gijón, my parents thought it wise for them to leave Spain. Around that time, Grossmama went to live with my father's close friend, Nicolas Sainz, and his wife in Becedas.

Grossmama with Nicolas Sainz and his wife in Becedas.

My father was a liberal and was therefore labeled "a leftist," which meant his beliefs were contrary to the conservative Nationalist forces fighting to overthrow the government. Spain was full of hate and persecutions from both the extreme right and the extreme left. Some friends informed my dad that the extreme left groups were suspicious of his German nationality and suspected him of espionage, so they advised him to leave Madrid. The hate generated from political and religious radicalization is difficult to explain to those fortunate enough to have never lived through it. It led to horrific acts, from burning churches to assassinations on the streets—and both sides were responsible.

Broken lives—our mother returns

After leaving Spain, my parents went to France, stopping in the town of Saint-Jean-de-Luz. Although we had also stopped there after being evacuated, sadly, we did not see them there because we had already left for Zamora, Spain, by then. After some time in France, my parents made the difficult decision that my mother would return to Gijón, Spain, to reunite with us at Abuelito's, but my father would remain in France since it was dangerous for him to return. We did not see him again for four years. Only later did we learn how much misfortune and adversity he endured during those long years. The separation was

Chapter 2: Family Life and War through the Eyes of a Child

difficult, and for a long time, we did not even know whether he was alive or dead.

World War II officially began in 1939, but it has always been my view that the Spanish Civil War was the precursor—the match that ignited the powder keg of the global war. My family had just lived through the Spanish conflict, and now, we were feeling the effects of Hitler's terrible actions since our name clearly showed a Jewish heritage. For Hitler, being Jewish was not a matter of religion but what he considered race—inherited from parents, regardless of religious affiliation or practice. Since my father was born 100 percent Jewish, Hitler would consider me and my siblings to be 50 percent Jewish, and my children today would be 25 percent Jewish. (Even though my mother was not Jewish, and despite the fact that my father converted, and we were practicing Catholics, by Hitler's definition, we would still be considered Jewish.)

While my father was in France with a German passport, Germany launched their invasion of France. My father's documents clearly indicated that he was born in Metz and chose not to become a French citizen in 1918—he had elected instead to continue being a German. (He had not felt it was honorable to change nationalities just because his "Fatherland" had lost the war.) Unfortunately, some twenty-plus years later, he was now suspected of being a German spy and was jailed in Paris because of that decision.

Shortly after WWII started in 1939, the Germans entered and occupied Paris, and all political prisoners, including my father, were "liberated". In order to survive, my father sold writing pens and wristwatches on the streets of Paris. Thanks to his fluency in German, the "occupiers" were regular clients, until he made an unfortunate sale to members of an intelligence unit. They asked my father for his documentation, and since he would not deny being "200 percent Jewish" (100 percent from his father and 100 percent from his mother, as he used to say half-jokingly), they sent him to a German concentration camp in France.

While in the concentration camp, he and several other prisoners were lucky enough to escape during a bombardment. Once the British were certain that my father was not a supporter of Hitler, he became a "volunteer" with the British army. Not long afterward, the Dunkirk catastrophe occurred, where the British forces had to flee France back to England. Since there was limited space on the British transport ships, there was no room for the new "volunteers," and the Brits' advice was, "You are all now civilians again—take your clothes and run. We have no room to evacuate you." My father started running toward the border of Spain.

Sometimes, when you are experiencing a difficult time, chess can be of help. Your games, your strategies, and your own personal universe allow your mind to avoid and forget the problems that weigh you down. My father knew this, and thanks to chess, he was able to endure truly challenging times…and there was no shortage of them. While waiting near the Spanish border, fleeing Hitler and the Gestapo, my father's life was rough. He survived by taking advantage of his previous experiences and skills—he gave classes in chess and languages. In those times of waiting and uncertainty while trying to return to us, chess was a great help. At night, he would play with friends in the cafes at the main plaza of the city, which provided relief from the tension he lived with day after day.

My father fully intended to re-enter Spain through the official channels, but unfortunately, he was repeatedly denied permission because he was undocumented—in 1940, Hitler had stripped all of us of our German nationality because we were Jews.

Chapter 2: Family Life and War through the Eyes of a Child

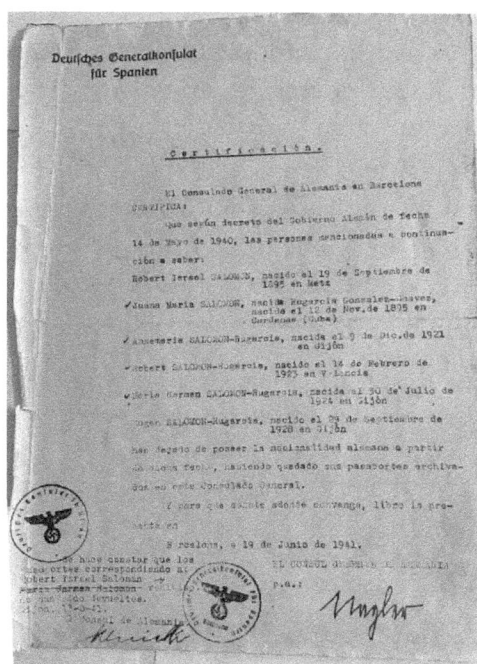

The letter from the German Consulate in Barcelona certifying that according to the government decree issued on May 14, 1940, Robert "Israel" Salomon and his family are no longer entitled to possess German citizenship from that day forward, and that our passports would be retained in the General Consulate's office in Barcelona.

After having been denied legal entrance to Spain because of his lack of documentation, and after several months in hiding near the France/Spain border, my father crossed the Pyrenees illegally with the help of a sympathetic Basque guide. As he was having his first breakfast in a coffee shop in Spain, two police officers came in, looked at him…and my father decided to turn himself in. The police officers took him to HQ and presented him to their commander, who wanted to return him to Hitler. My father asked him not to, asking instead, "Can you do me one last favor before then?" The commander agreed. "I want you to give me your word of honor." Yes, the commander again agreed. My father said, "I want you to shoot me right here, so I can die in Spain, where I have a wife and four children. I do not want to die in Hitler's hands."

Having already given my father his word, the colonel consulted with another military officer about the situation. The colonel returned to tell my father and said, "Since you have a family in Spain, we will treat you as an undocumented alien, but we must send you to a concentration camp. Do you agree?" Yes, my father consented. Fortunately, this was a camp for foreigners escaping the war (i.e., undocumented citizens), and there were many notable prisoners: musicians, writers, etc. Chess was very helpful in this concentration camp—my father played chess, and he taught fellow prisoners to play.

It took several months, but with the help of my mother's family (who were well connected with the "religious right"), my father was freed, provided that he would leave the country. This allowed our family to finally be together again for a few months, which, to a child's perception, was only a fleeting moment.

Left: 1941—The family was back together, an infrequent occurrence.
Right: Family picture taken in 1943 just before my father left for Cuba. It was taken at his request on the farm where he lived when he first came to Spain—he would play his cello right on that spot.

As a condition for his release from the concentration camp, my father had to leave Spain. He decided to go to Cuba where there were still some distant cousins of my mother and applied for Cuban citizenship. The process was slow…and my father, along with the family, was in no hurry. Eventually, however, his continued presence in Spain came to the attention of the authorities. They were so enraged that they sent him to a second concentration camp to wait until he presented the official permit to travel to Cuba.

Obviously, that brought home the sense of urgency, and when he finally received his Cuban citizenship papers in 1943, my father left for Havana soon afterward, unfortunately, during a time when

Chapter 2: Family Life and War through the Eyes of a Child

German submarines were torpedoing ships in the Atlantic. My brother, Roberto, who by then was a medical student at Madrid University, decided to accompany my father to help him to survive adversity and to prepare to reunite the family. It was an inspirational lesson from my older brother about the priority of family. In my mind and heart, he was a true unsung hero.

I knew that my father had to leave, but that did not make it any easier. I was fourteen years old, and except for a few months, I hadn't been with my father since 1936. Seven years—an eternity in the life of a child. Due to his exile from Spain, it would be four more years before I would see him again. In total, the war and its consequences separated me from my father for ten years. Those were ten critical years, because the importance of a father figure in the life of a child cannot be overstated.

The beginning of a separation

Can a war divide a family? The war itself, probably not, but could the radicalization of political and religious beliefs fuel a civil war? Yes, definitely.

Eighty years later, I now understand that my mother's family was *"de derechas"* (rich, politically right-leaning, and conservative). My father, on the other hand, was a firm believer in social justice, which at the time was considered *"de izquierdas"* (politically leftist and liberal). Our family was considered "middle-right" politically.

As I said, my mother came from the wealthy, Catholic conservative Rugarcía family. In contrast, my father's brother Max fought for the German army during World War I and was sent to the Russian front. I suppose his time in Russia from 1916 to '17, as a prisoner of war, may have skewed his vision of the world. The things he saw and heard there presumably influenced his political beliefs, making him into an extreme leftist. Max married Concha Cazalis, whose family was also left-leaning. On one side of the family (an ideological divide), were the four Salomon Rugarcía children of Robert and Juana, and on the other side were the two Salomon Cazalis children of Max and Concha. We were six children who, concerned only with playing and childhood

37

pursuits, could not have imagined that in a few years, we would be separated by ideas we could not begin to understand.

Due to their ideological and political differences, brothers Robert and Max were eventually on opposite sides of the Spanish Civil War. (The Republican forces were supporters of the democratically elected president of the Second Spanish Republic, while General Francisco Franco led the Nationalist forces.) Robert's family was considered to be politically right-leaning, while Max, a leftist, supported the Republican forces. Alongside a group of friends, he took to the mountains surrounding the capital to form a brigade whose mission was to defend Madrid against the advance of the Nationalist troops. He was unquestionably successful in his mission—even the press announced his deeds, finally dubbing him "the German Jew who saved Madrid." (Many years later, in a village near where he was wounded, Buitrago de Lozoya, that rocky spot of the Madrid mountains was officially named "*La Pena del Aleman*," The Rock of the German, as an homage to Max for his heroism and success.)

The conflict ran its course and ended with a Nationalist victory, counting my uncle among the lucky volunteer leftist brigades who managed to survive. Max and his family needed to flee Spain as quickly as possible, so they went to France. However, France was not a place for a leftist militant, especially not a Jewish one, so they then fled to the Dominican Republic where he found work on a farm. Those were difficult years of exhausting work with little pay. Max eventually became so worried about his children's future that, with the help of an old friend from the militia who was living in Mexico, he obtained the necessary travel visas and settled his family in Mexico, where their situation improved. Sadly, along the way, the ties between the two brothers and their families were broken by seemingly irreconcilable political beliefs, resulting in a twenty-four-year separation.

The politics of the Spanish Civil War had completely separated my family, and we had to begin a brand-new story, entirely different from life prior to the war. It was to be a life where six cousins, from two politically opposite families, would lose their childhood and be scattered across the globe, unable to get together until twenty-five years later.

Chess as a refuge

The Spanish Civil War had finally passed, but we were now faced with the difficult post-war era. We were one of the lucky families who hadn't had anyone killed in the war, but we were among the thousands of families who suffered the brutal consequences of that cruel war for years afterward. (Now, eighty years later, I think about what my father wrote in his book, *Walking and Wondering*, and I cannot help but wonder how it is possible that political and ideological hate could negate the natural blood ties of family and love. I can see a similar situation developing in this country, one of polarization and political divide, and I am worried for my grandchildren. The Civil War in Spain resulted in 500,000 dead, in a country that at the time was not even 10 percent of today's US population.)

We continued to live in the house on San Bernardo St. in Gijón, with Abuelito, where I had learned about chess from my first teacher—my father. During our brief reunion with him in 1941 (when he was released from the concentration camp, under the condition to leave Spain), we spent hours together every evening playing chess. At that time, I hadn't seen him in five years, and we knew he had to go soon, which was heartbreaking. While we played, he told me stories about his adventures and shared his ideals and vision of the world. I believe he used chess to create a bond with me, his youngest son, who had missed him during the critical ages of seven to thirteen years.

In reality, we were starting to get to know each other. (Before the separation in 1936, I was still too young for us to create a normal father-son bond.) We shared many nights of chess during those precious few months, so you can imagine and understand what it represents for me, and why the game holds a position of such importance in my life. In the difficult years that followed, I believe that chess was a refuge for me as well, a place to which I could escape and where I could have everything under control.

CHAPTER 3:
My Intense Chess Life
(1943–1947)

World War II was ending, but my family seemed to be coming apart at the seams. My Abuela Juana (my maternal grandmother) had taken a bad fall and died before the Spanish Civil War, and Abuelito passed away in late 1943. Grossmama (my paternal grandmother) was living with the Sainz family in Becedas (and would pass away shortly thereafter). My father and brother were about to leave for Cuba, and what was left of my nuclear family was trying to pick up the pieces of our lives. Chess was about to become a major part of my life, and I had my father and my uncle to thank for it.

My first steps on the board

My father had not limited himself to simply teaching me how to play chess. He also tried to pass on his passion for this game to me, an endeavor in which he was unquestionably successful. Chess has accompanied me throughout my life and has given me many happy hours. In my first steps, the chess giants Capablanca, Lasker, and Alekhine were by my side. I replayed dozens of their games, and thanks to the Cuban (Capablanca), I fell in love with endgames, a phase of the game that greatly helped me to succeed for many years. It was Alekhine, however, with his enormous creative talent who impressed me the most, to the point that he became my idol.

When my father couldn't teach me anymore, reinforcements

arrived. My uncle Casimiro Rugarcía (a well-known doctor who became Alekhine's personal physician during his stay in Gijón), was a strong amateur, and by his side, I was able to improve my game. He helped me to go deeper into the beautiful world of combinations, discovering that creativity can be developed on a chessboard in almost unlimited ways.

When my uncle considered that I had reached the necessary level, he began to take me to his club, *Casino de la Unión de los Gremios*, where some of the strongest players in Gijón would meet to play chess. Manuel de las Clotas and Antonio Rico would show up from time to time there; the professor/writer Juan Fernández Rúa, along with Dr. Salas or the very strong Vicente González, also attended more regularly. Overseeing all activities was the great chess organizer and future president of Spain's Chess Federation, Félix de las Heras. I also had frequent contact with other strong players such as Mampel and Bonet and learned a great deal from all of them, so I continued to improve.

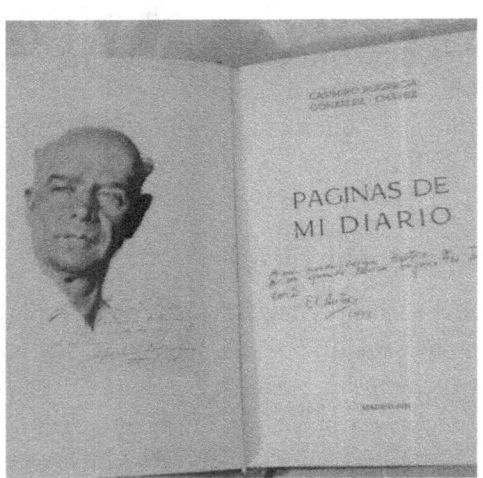

My Uncle Casi's book of poems, with a touching dedication to Bea and myself. This book is one of my greatest treasures and has been on my night table since he gave it to me in 1971. The picture is a reproduction of a painting by a very famous Spanish painter Segura.

My "Uncle Casi" was a multi-talented individual, an excellent singer, a painter, a poet, and a great fan of chess. Before beginning his career in medicine, he spent time in Italy to take advanced painting courses and train his tenor voice. He did marry, but the marriage didn't last, which may have pushed him toward chess. Uncle Casi had the soul of an artist and used the board as another canvas upon which to create beauty. He always played with passion, and at times the game consumed him, leading to some humorous moments. On one occasion, he was so absorbed in his game that he threw a pawn he had just captured into his coffee and stirred it as if it was a lump of sugar.

1943: My first successes

I fondly remember my first appearances in the Gijón competitive chess scene; we took a pleasant trip in 1943 to Oviedo with the local chess team from the *"Casino"* led by the great chess organizer Felix de las Heras. (We defeated the Oviedo team and, by winning my game, I became a hero).

The year 1943 was an interesting one. I won my first tournament, a third category (beginners) competition sponsored by the *"Educación y Descanso,"* a government department created by the Franco regime to facilitate recreational activities. That success allowed me to move up to the second category. Only a month later, I finished second in a tournament in my new category, just one half a point behind the winner, José Luis García Leicher. I spent many chess afternoons with Leicher; with the board and pieces under our arms, we would take the tram to Somió Park, where we would find a bench and play games endlessly.

That same year, I got my first win against a renowned master. José Sanz Aguado had just become Spanish champion and gave a simultaneous exhibition in Gijón. I was fourteen years old, and at that time, the chess world was so captivated by the Arturito Pomar phenomenon that people used to fantasize about the appearance of new child prodigies. After defeating Sanz Aguado (the very recent new Champion of Spain), the Madrid newspaper *El Alcázar* published this article on August 11, 1943: The headline reads, "Another Arturito Pomar has arrived.

His name is Salomón, he is 14 years old and he has already defeated Champion Sanz."

I suppose that those difficult years of the postwar period and the brief but intense few months spent with my father were the start of my lifelong admiration for him, as well as my eighty years of passion for chess. Thanks to the success in Oviedo with the team from Gijón's *Casino de los Gremios*, the subsequent tournament wins that allowed me to advance in level, and my win against Spanish champion Sanz Aguado, I had made quite a name for myself in Gijón.

At the end of that summer, the chess environment of Gijón was about to be changed forever. As was his custom each afternoon, my uncle, Dr. Casimiro Rugarcía, was playing against Dr. Pedro del Río, president of *"El Casino de la Unión de los Gremios"*. On this day, I had accompanied my uncle, and I could see that Félix de las Heras, the great chess organizer, had entered the casino in such a state of excitement that we knew something important was happening. He approached the table and stopped the game by informing the president that he had received an offer from World Chess Champion Alexander Alekhine: If an international tournament was organized in Gijón, the world champion would participate. Thus, the Gijón International Tournament was born, first played in July of 1944.

Of course, Alekhine was not at the same level as in his glory days of the 1920s, when he defeated Capablanca to become World Champion in 1927 and won most of the tournaments he entered. The years had taken their toll, and his addiction to alcohol had not helped...but he was still Alekhine, and we were going to be able to see him in a tournament in our hometown!

In addition to Alekhine, the organization managed to attract two other big names, Antonio Medina and Arturo Pomar, along with the most outstanding players from Gijón (Vicente González, Antonio Rico, Arturo Bonet, Miguel Mampel, Gallego, and Dr. Salas). The turnout for the competition was extraordinary; fans packed the room every day, forcing the organizers to install a chessboard outside for people who were not fortunate enough to get in. This allowed everyone to witness how Alekhine dominated the competition with an iron fist, surpassing an inspired Medina by one point and yielding his only draw against twelve-year-old child prodigy Arturo "Arturito" Pomar (who would later become my friend).

I experienced the entire event, the First International Chess Tournament of Gijón (1944), with great excitement and enthusiasm, and even managed to work my way into being a "gofer" for the tournament. I was there to help wherever they needed me by placing the pieces or making sure that each player had water, coffee, or whatever was necessary.

Impulsively, sensing that I was facing a unique opportunity, I begged my mother to buy me a new chess set. (I intended to place my own pieces on the board where Alekhine had to play.) My plan worked, and those pieces became one of my most prized possessions and have accompanied me through all these years, wherever I have gone.

Standing: Eugene Salomon (L) and Juan Fernández Rúa (R) **Seated:** Félix de las Heras, Alexander Alekhine, Dr. Muñiz, and his son.

A few days before the competition, something happened that changed my life. It was a hot afternoon in July (a rare occurrence in Gijón), and the time had come for Alekhine to return to his hotel. My uncle, being aware that Alekhine had drunk more than necessary, asked me to accompany him.

"We must not let him go alone," he discreetly advised.

And so, we left, the chess champion of the world and me, walking down Corrida Street arm-in-arm toward the Hotel Comercio, where he was staying. I was just a boy, and I suppose that Alekhine perceived in me a huge love for chess, so he decided to give me some advice that would remain with me for the rest of my days.

"Young man, chess is not something to which one should dedicate his entire life."

I embraced and followed Alekhine's advice and have passed it on to my children as part of "the rules of the house" they had to follow. They needed to be bilingual, study piano for four years, and, even if they became passionate about chess, they should not make it their profession...advice they have followed faithfully.

A few weeks later, Alekhine was again in front of me, but this time as an opponent across the board. He was giving an exhibition, playing ten boards simultaneously with a clock, against the most prominent players in the city. Because I had already made quite a name for myself as a child prodigy in Gijón, I was selected to be one of Alekhine's opponents in this ten-board simultaneous exhibition.

There I was, a fifteen-year-old, joyful and awestruck, playing against my idol. Alekhine won game after game, but still, I held on in an evenly matched position where I had a serious chance of achieving a draw. All my teammates had already lost their games, but I continued head-to-head with Alekhine until I eventually conceded the game. The commentators opined that the position should have ended in a draw, but I guess it was not meant to be.

This game, and my walk with my chess idol on the *Calle Corrida* (Corrida Street) in my hometown, impacted my life on both boards—the chessboard as well as the board of life. As a fifteen-year-old, the world champion's comment about the role of chess in life remained with me forever. Over the next fifty years, I have repeated his advice many times, not only to the many students that I helped to train as a high school coach but also to the chess clubs where I was a guest speaker. In my lecturing about chess, I frequently used this game, as well as examples from my games involving combinations and endings.

Madrid, the city of my dreams

Our post-war, year-round life in Gijón with Abuelito came to an end when my family returned to Madrid at the end of 1943. My grandfather had lost his whole fortune as a consequence of the Civil War, and we couldn't keep living there and having him support us. We needed to be back on our own and had to organize our life.

It could not have been easy for my mother, raising four children by herself. During this time, she had to be both father and mother for us, but she rarely complained even though life was a struggle. My two sisters took an intensive secretarial course (typing and stenography) and found jobs. (As an anecdote from those days, I remember that in order to practice, Mela would transcribe the ongoing dinner table conversation with her finger in the air.) Seeing her daughters forced to work to maintain the family (and having sisters who were secretaries) was sad for my mother to watch. It was also, in those days, a sudden come down on the social scale, and a blow to the social standing of the family.

After all the family's assets were sold, my mother even had to sell her personal jewelry to supplement the money my sisters were earning in order to survive. Having been raised in a rich family, this was a trauma for her. She would occasionally refer to "lucky friends" whose husbands were non-political and who had not taken risks to help people in need, but she loved my father and stuck by him. My teenage years were tough, but the memories of my youth are still beautiful.

When my mother, sisters, and I returned to live in Madrid in September 1943, I was already a strong chess player. However, Madrid was a much bigger city and a much bigger challenge on the board, and there would be many more to come. They happened in different places, different countries, and lasted for decades, and they all provided unforgettable experiences.

Sweet Memories — Family, Friends, Chess, and Sugar

My class at the Jovellanos Institute. I am in the second row, the seventh from the left.... Curiously enough, in the same row, fourth from the left is the teacher of physics, Maria Luisa Menendez Rugarcía, my dear cousin from whom I had learned to love poetry during the war at age seven. Coincidences!!

Back in Gijón, I had completed my fourth year of high school at the "*Instituto Jovellanos.*" (In those times in Spain, high school was seven years of study, typically from age ten to age seventeen). Once in Madrid, I was accepted at the *Ramiro de Maeztu*, a prestigious "model school" of the Spanish government. I imagine that friends of my mother's family were responsible for getting me accepted there.

Every summer, however, we still returned to Gijón, and to its chess activities. It was there that a friendship began, which was strengthened across a chessboard.

Román Torán and the summers of the sixty-four squares

Román Torán Albero is a well-known figure in Spanish chess. He began by carving out a great reputation as a player, achieving many successes and frequently competing outside of Spain. He later served as vice president of FIDE, distinguishing himself as a leader, and became an important figure in the growth of chess in Spain.

Torán's first steps on the board can be traced to when he lived in

Alcoy, a town in the southeast of Spain, about 250 miles from Madrid. As an adolescent, his play was already dazzling, and he enjoyed a great deal of success at the regional (province) level. As Torán himself tells it, even though his passion for chess had appeared years earlier, his time in Gijón (when he witnessed Alekhine's simuls in November of 1943) left an indelible mark on his life. From that day on, Torán devoured every chess book that fell into his hands, allowing him to progress steadily, even though he was always in the shadow of Arturo Pomar, who was the same age as he was.

During those years, chess pieces were in stiff competition with soccer balls. Torán was an outstandingly fast right wing for the Alcoy soccer team, but after a rival's kick left his knee badly injured, he turned his full attention to chess, to which he dedicated his life. When he returned to Gijón, he decided to become a professional chess player, telling an interviewer, "…It's a good profession, chess player…calm, and it allows you to see the world. I would prefer to do nothing, but that is not possible." During that time, Torán wrote a chess column in two national newspapers, *Arriba* and *La Vanguardia*, brought in foreign chess books to distribute them throughout the country, and founded a chess academy. As he improved as a player, he beat both Pomar and Medina and won two national titles (1951 and 1953).

As a teenager in 1944 and 1945, I shared many afternoons of chess with Torán, who was living in Gijón, where my family spent their summers. That enabled us to meet and develop a good friendship by playing friendly games and analyzing openings. I was two years older than him, and I often won. I am pretty sure no one else had as good a score against Torán as I did!

As the years passed, I stayed in touch with Torán, always visiting him whenever I traveled to Madrid. The last time we were together, he invited us to dinner at his house, and he showed me his latest endeavor—the magazine "*Ocho x Ocho*" (*Eight by Eight*), whose main office was in the apartment next to his. He was quite proud of his accomplishments and was certainly an extremely successful individual.

I also met Arturito Pomar during this time, almost at the same time as he met Román Torán. It happened in Gijón, during the first international tournament, where Arturito was one of the participants. I was fifteen, he was thirteen, and we met during a meal in honor of Alekhine. The event was in Somió Park, and after the luncheon, we organized a friendly soccer match.

Pomar is the one in short pants, and I am the only one wearing a white jacket.

Torán was the same age as Pomar, and they also met during the tournament of 1944. Toran admitted that, despite knowing almost nothing about chess in those days, he followed Pomar's games with great interest and became Pomar's biggest fan. They shared afternoons playing barefoot soccer on the beach of San Lorenzo and swapping El Coyote books. Torán once wrote about how they met:

"I approached him to ask about the result of his game, and he answered me saying, 'Today I lost...yes.' I wanted to console him, but I couldn't think of anything better than, 'Tomorrow we will win.' We laughed and I invited him to go to the beach together."

In the mid-1940s, chess was a very important part of my life. I prepared intensely and dedicated a great deal of time to its study, and my level rose steadily. In the summer of 1945, I was able to put myself to the test on several occasions against the most outstanding players of Gijón, usually in rapid games. According to the records in my pocket notebook of the time, I beat Juan Fernández Rúa 2-0, drew a match (+2-2) with the excellent Manuel de las Clotas, and beat Vicente González 3-2. In addition, I defeated Torán in a long match 9-3 (+8 = 2-2) and ended the summer beating the Portuguese master, Francisco Lupi, 8.5-4.5 (+7 = 3-3). Despite all that, I did not dedicate too much time to my theoretical openings preparation and often played them

Chapter 3: My Intense Chess Life

far off from theory, trying to confuse my rivals, especially the most theoretical ones like Ganzo and Torán.

In Madrid, my "chess fever" reached its high point. I played tournaments and practiced around the clock, which resulted in several wins, such as the provincial (regional) *La Granja* Tournament (where I faced rivals such as Toledano, Alba, and Leicher), and my win at the *La Isla* Tournament in first category (the strongest section of players in the tournament).

La Isla Tournament: 1st category (April 1944)

Semifinals
1- Eugene Salomon
2- Baonza
3- José Luis Gª Leicher
4- Prytz

Final
1- Eugene Salomon
2- Pérez Bejarano
3- Brígido Chamero
4- Antonio De Alba

In 1945, I participated in the semifinals of the regional championship of Castile, Spain (Madrid and surrounding provinces). As luck would have it, in the semi-finals, in my group, I had to contend not only with Bové, a very strong Madrid player, but also with the phenomenal Arturito Pomar, the child prodigy that would become Spain's first ever grandmaster. Only three players from the group would go into the finals. Well, Bové finished in first place with 5.5 points after giving up only one draw (to me). I finished in second with five points, and Pomar ended up in third place after losing to Bove and drawing with me. In the finals, however, I received quite a reality check: Arturito Pomar had a sensational win.

My game with Pomar in the finals was interesting but had to be postponed when the time limit for the session was reached. Somebody told me that during the adjournment, Alekhine, former world champion and Pomar's teacher at that time, had helped him to analyze the ending, leading to a hard-fought win for my opponent.

The finals were the confirmation of Pomar as a phenomenon. He was proclaimed champion of Castile with great brilliancy. I did not have a great result, finishing in ninth place. It was a valuable and humbling lesson, one I probably needed at my age.

Enrolled at Club Maudes

In the 1940s, Juan Manuel Fuentes headed a chess club that met at the cafe *Granja el Henar*, on Alcalá St. in Madrid. I joined the group within a few days of arriving in Madrid on the recommendation of José Luis García Leicher, who had also recently moved from Gijón to Madrid.

Several months later, Fuentes (who was deaf) started a chess club for those with disabilities, sponsored by *Educación y Descanso* (a government agency dedicated to promoting cultural and recreational activities). Since many blind players frequented the club, the pieces had a nail in the top to distinguish the black pieces from the white ones. All of us from the club of *Granja El Henar* joined the new club, which was located on busy San Jerónimo St., very near the famous *Puerta del Sol* plaza in the center of Madrid. In 1945, with Fuentes at the helm, the club moved to the *Hogar del Trabajador* building, located within walking distance of my home (at the corner of Alonso Cano and Martinez Campos streets). A new club was born, and many players, including myself and my good friend Víctor García Queimadelos, joined the group.

(The Spanish chess historian, Jesus Remis Fernandez, has compiled a wonderfully comprehensive text about the history of Madrid's Maudes Chess Club on the website *Historia del ajedrez español*, titled *Hogar del Productor Maudes de Educación y Descanso*. It was emotional reading, not only because it was about a wonderful club but also because the author dedicated the article to me! "*A Eugene Salomón Rugarcía uno de aquellos héroes supervivientes*" —To Eugene Salomon Rugarcía—one of the surviving heroes. I felt, and still feel, incredibly honored.)

For many years, Fuentes was one of the top players in Spain. I guess that he had heard the story of my father being in exile in Cuba, and he was always most friendly and helpful to me. He was a true friend, projecting a "father-like" image to this then-sixteen-year-old.

Later on, we had one of the most remarkable players of the time (Francisco Jose Perez) join our Maudes club. I tremendously enjoyed playing tournaments and training matches against him as well as analyzing the Colle System and the Alekhine Defense with him.

The club was not exclusively for chess; when one entered the doors, you always found several workers playing *mus* (a card game). We chess players did not stop amid the card playing—we went upstairs to the first floor, where the chessboards and pieces were ready and waiting for us. There, we played games, analyzed positions and openings, challenged ourselves, and played training tournaments.

It is remarkable for me to remember the time the strong German player, Hermann Seeger, just before returning to Germany, invited me for a beer one afternoon. He was a tall, strong man, and I had always suspected that he was a German agent...and I was Jewish. We stopped into the first tavern we found, and once we got our drinks, he told me that he simply wanted to say goodbye to me. His country had just lost the war, and he felt obligated to go back and help with the reconstruction. He said that it had been a pleasure to meet and play chess with me. We shook hands firmly; I wished him well and returned to the club. Knowing that I was Jewish, had he just asked for forgiveness for what his country had done?

Aside from those already mentioned, the club had several well-known players from Madrid such as Toledano, Palacios, and Rubio (who would later become champion of Uruguay). Julio Ganzo would also turn up at the club often, even though he played for the "*Real Madrid*" team and was never a member of our team. In 1946, we won a great victory in the team championship in Castile. With F.J. Perez on first board, Queimadelos on second, myself on third, and Fuentes on fourth, we won first place, beating the incredibly strong team from Real Madrid (with Pomar, Sanz, Reborio, and Ganzo) who finished in second.

Also in 1946, at age eighteen, I was a reserve player for the Spanish team that faced Argentina in a radio match on October 12, 1946, which Spain won in a close match. Although I did not get to play (since none of the team members dropped out), I greatly enjoyed the event and being present the whole night. The match lasted until the wee hours of the morning due to the time difference between the two countries. That same year, I began my studies in medicine, but my time in that discipline would be short. Víctor Manuel García Queimadelos was not only a fellow member of *Club Maudes* and a classmate in the school of medicine, but he was also one of my best friends, which continued as the years passed. As first-year students in medicine, we attended anatomy class in the old "*Escuela de San Carlos*" in a big, dark classroom where the professor constantly projected slides. Queima and I, who always sat in the back, often had odd, whispered conversations: "1.P-4R, N-3AR; 2.P-5R, N-4D...." As you may have already noticed, it had to do with Alekhine's Defense. We always played at least two games of blindfold chess every class.

In the *Glorieta de la Iglesia* cafe next to my house, between bites of appetizers and with pints of beer in hand, we dreamed of curing cancer one day. Victor became a famous oncologist at *Fundación Jiménez Díaz* hospital in Madrid, as well as one of the strongest chess players in the capital. He became champion of Castile in 1953 and continued to win outstanding victories such as his first-place finish at the 1954 International Tournament of Madrid (where he beat Lodewijk Prins, Bordell, and Díez del Corral).

Over the years, Queima and I shared some of fate's roadblocks: He also abandoned chess for many years, thirteen in total, returning successfully in 1975 during the Aviaco Open, where he finished second behind Gete. One thing he never abandoned was our friendship, which persisted despite the distance and the passage of time.

My most important tournament: Gijón 1947

Without a doubt, the most important competition I ever took part in was the Fourth International Tournament of Gijón. It was a magnificent experience: playing in my city and doing it against some of the strongest players in Spain, the Dutch player Lodewijk Prins, and the British player Harold Baruch Wood (who was a last-minute substitution for Sir George Alan Thomas). For me, it was a new experience, playing in an international tournament whose birth I had witnessed. There I was, as a teenager, in an atmosphere of seriousness that surrounds the greatest events.

Francisco José Pérez (left) vs Eugene Salomon, Gijón 1947

Just three years earlier, I had placed the pieces for Alekhine to move, and now, here I was—from a "gofer" to a player. The chosen location could not have been better: the "*Real Club Astur de Regatas*" (Royal Yacht Club of Asturias), an elegant and spacious site, ideal for playing chess. (Sixty-two years later, I would return there, to the very same room, to play an international bridge tournament with my nephew Roberto as my partner...but that is another story.)

Once again, the tireless Felix de las Heras led the organization and did so with obvious success. Pérez and Prins were neck and neck up until the final and finished tied for first in the classification, splitting the prize money for first and second place (1,500 and 1,000 pesetas). Every participant received different prizes that had been donated by the merchants of Gijón. I did well against the players who finished in the top five spots. No one was able to defeat me, and I won an important victory against Medina—a game that was considered one of the greatest surprises of the tournament by the journalists.

The youngsters of the tournament: Pablo Morán, Arturito Pomar, Eugene Salomon, Ramón del Olmo, and Román Torán

Just a few days after the tournament, I received congratulations from my father…in Havana, Cuba. He was proud to hear that his "student" had beaten the champion of Spain! It was thrilling, but it also put into focus that our family was still separated and that getting together was the real goal.

CHAPTER 4:
A New Life in Cuba
(1947–1953)

In the late 1940s, the situation in Spain after the war was not promising. On top of that, the family was split in two by the Atlantic Ocean, and we needed to find a way to reunite, which was not going to be easy.

My father and brother, trying not to worry us, never told us about the difficulties they faced during those years in Cuba, but I know they lived in a small, rented room where all that was provided was one double bed. In April of 1946, after three years of exile and hard work in Cuba, my father and brother had enough savings to buy a transatlantic ticket for my sister Ana Maria in 1946, and she left for Havana. She left Spain to reunite with them, and things began to improve. My father (who had been a paid cellist in the Havana Philharmonic Orchestra) started selling watches; my brother, after two years working at the large department store *La Filosofía* became an assistant to congressman Angel "*El Curita*" (the Little Priest) Fernández Varela, while Ana María got a job as a stenographer-typist in a government office.

With prospects improving, the possibility that the entire family could reunite began to take shape. For the moment, my mother could not make the trip (my sister Mela would be getting married in a few months, and she would stay in Madrid); so, it was my turn to leave Spain toward the unknown Caribbean. November 2, 1947, found me at the port of Cadiz, Spain. Cadiz, known as "*La Tacita de Plata*" (The Little Silver Cup), resembles Havana, and I was about to discover that. I was ready to board the *Magallanes*, a transatlantic ship, to Cuba and my new life. My mother could not come to see me off, but she managed to contact a friend in Cádiz who, with her young son, took me around town on a horse-drawn carriage. When she hugged me goodbye, I could feel my mother's love through the tears that flooded the eyes of her friend, Marita.

Left: My brother Roberto (left) with Robert Salomon, our father. **Right:** Me, on my arrival to Cuba, November 1947

She also gave me a lovely surprise—a leather-bound copy of *Las Mil Mejores Poesías de la Lengua Española* (*The 1,000 Greatest Poems of the Spanish Language*), with an inscription to me by my cousin/godmother, "Chuqui" (Maria Herminia), dated "Cadiz 1947". Somehow, my godmother had found a way to send the book to Marita, who brought me so much comfort and the love of family farewell as I departed for Havana. To this day, I still keep that book on my bedside table, a seventy-five-year companion!

That same night, we set sail for Havana, where my father, brother, and sister awaited me. I was only nineteen years old, and I was dealing with a gigantic change, leaving behind my roots, and facing life in a new country with a future full of unknowns.

I had a lot of time to wonder what my new life would bring since the trip took three weeks. The nights were a peaceful darkness, with a sky full of stars such as I had never seen before in my life. I remember one truly complicated moment when we reached the latitude of Terra

Chapter 4: A New Life in Cuba

Nova, Newfoundland, and were surprised by a hurricane with winds of ninety miles per hour. For a time, we feared the worst.

Due to the problems we had with the storm, we needed to make a one-day stop in New York. For me, without a visa to disembark in New York, it was just the first opportunity to see the famous Statue of Liberty, at the entry to NY—an eternal symbol of freedom in the land of immigrants! (There was also another much sweeter moment—a brief and fleeting romance in the middle of the ocean with a young lady, also from Spain.)

Finally, we sighted Havana, and were surrounded by flying fish who leaped so high that they seemed to be flying. Those fish, shaped like torpedoes, jumped out of the water so forcefully that they resembled projectiles, and their jumps were so high that it was truly impressive.

At the port of Havana, my father and brother smilingly greeted me. It was emotional, but at the same time, I imagine that I was wondering: Here we are, some two hundred immigrants… What does destiny have in store for us? Turns out that for me, it would be thirteen beautiful years in Cuba full of extremely hard work, university graduation, lifelong friendships, and a successful professional life. Those years would only include one year of chess (1952) but would prepare me to become a Grandmaster…not in chess, but as master of my own life. I had no way of knowing that thirteen years later, I would again be an immigrant, being welcomed again by the benevolent arms of the same Statue of Liberty I had first seen in 1947.

Happily reunited with my father and brother, we began walking toward the apartment of close friends, passing through Havana's historic Cathedral Plaza. After some relaxation, we continued to the rented modest flat where they lived far from the city, in the *Nuevo Vedado* section. Their flat was very close to the bridge over the Almendares River, the very same river after which Abuelito's estate was named. This name transported me back to the happy memories of our childhood, and I was even happier that I was able to hug my sister Ana María again.

I still remember with a smile meeting my brother's beautiful girlfriend, Marisa. She looked at me and said to my brother, "*Está como platanito para sinsonte*," (he is like a small banana for a mockingbird)—a very Cuban phrase meaning something (or someone) very attractive. I had no idea what a "*sinsonte*" was, so I did not initially understand that her comment was one of the nicest things she could say about me. That compliment still makes me smile, seventy-five years later.

At sunset, we met up with Congressman Angel Fernández Varela, boss and good friend of Roberto, who had offered to show me Havana. The drive ended at a popular café, *Los Aires Libres* at the corner of 12th & 23rd, where I drank, on the recommendation of my brother, my first vanilla milkshake, something that did not exist at that time in Spain. To this day, it is still one of my favorite drinks.

At the café, something happened that I did not initially consider important, but that later was revealed to be an incredible coincidence. While we were conversing, two young men entered the place. When he saw them, Angel raised his hand and waved them over. They sat down with us and started an animated conversation, through which we found out that one of them had been Angel's student at Belén Jesuit High School. The chat was interesting, and after they left, I asked Angel who his friend was.

He replied, "Eugene, that young man was one of my brightest students and has become a student leader at Havana University. Remember his name." Since I was headed for Havana University, I made it a point to remember the young man's name: It was Fidel Castro.

My faith and my first job

In the situation we were in, so far from home, it was clear that we all needed to pitch in and share the burden, so it was necessary for me to find a job. Curiously, my faith played a key role in that job search.

I had only been in Havana one week, and Roberto had introduced me to his second home away from home, the *Agrupación Católica Universitaria*, where he was an active member. In Madrid, I had been a very devout member of the congregation of the Virgin of the Miraculous Medal at the church of the Pauline Brothers, which was near my house. There, I would often play ping-pong in one of the rooms on an upper floor, and even more often, at sunset, I would kneel in one of the last rows and raise my eyes to God. It was like Núñez de Arce wrote in his famous poem, *Tristezas*:

> *"When I remember the sincere piety with which, I, in my youth, entered our old cathedrals,*
> *Where, kneeling down before the cross I raised my eyes to God, dreaming of heavenly happiness…"*

This poem perfectly reflects my situation and the nostalgia that I feel today in my old age.

It was there, in that group that we called the ACU that I found refuge and made lifelong friends. It was also thanks to the ACU that I got my first job in Havana…never suspecting the impact it would have on my life. It all happened when someone in the group told me I should go immediately to the *Colegio de Belén* and speak to Brother Feliz because there was a family that had just arrived from Spain. Two of their sons (one was a freshman in high school and the other was a junior) needed a teacher who could teach daily classes in subjects that were studied in high school in Spain. In Cuba, there weren't many people who had completed high school in Spain, so I was the ideal person for the job.

So, with Brother Feliz's recommendation, in January of 1948, I got my first job: teacher/tutor of the brothers Fernando and Javier Zulueta, sons of Julián Zulueta. My work was not limited to just teaching; rather, I was more than that. I helped with their education and traveled with the family when they had to travel to their sugar mill, *Central Zaza*, in Las Villas, in the outskirts of the town of Placetas. Through this position, I developed a great friendship with the family, which has remained intact even during years when we lived in different countries. True friendships know no borders.

Three Salomons in Cuba: Roberto, Robert, and Eugene (1947)

I recall that before starting my new job, our family was able to take a short Christmas vacation, and we traveled to San José del Lago, in Mayagigua, central Cuba. There, I discovered a delicious drink called "*España en llamas*" (Spain on Fire, made with champagne cider and cognac) and experienced for the first time—and the last! —what it is to be drunk. I remember my brother bringing me to my room and putting me in the shower, where I fell…while continuing to verbally play the game of dominos from that afternoon, saying, "*Me doblo— vaya si estaba doblado, jorobado.*" (In Spanish, *doblado* means both using a double tile in dominoes as well as to double over. I was so "*doblado*" from my drinking that I was almost a "*jorobado*"—a hunchback. It seemed downright hilarious at the time, but overall, however, it was not a good night, and I never repeated it.)

Several weeks later, we were able to move out of our very modest flat, near a garage and far from the city, to a new place that could be considered "middle class." This one was in the center of Havana, very near the university and the ACU and only two blocks from the Capablanca Chess Club.

When my first job finally began, I learned that my new boss, Julián Zulueta, was originally from San Sebastián, Spain (only about 225 miles from my native town of Gijón), and had come to Cuba to take charge of his family's *ingenio* (sugar mill). He soon expanded the business, acquiring the *Central Fe* factory, near Camajuaní. He then made a brilliant decision—he bought a small bank in Havana, the *Banco Ultramar*, which he would use to finance his sugar production. One morning, when he had called for me to discuss his sons' progress, he told me his plans for the future. "No one knows, but I have a great deal of experience after working in banks in England. I know what Cuba needs right now—a bank with branches throughout the country." He eventually converted *Banco Ultramar* into *Banco Continental Cubano*, the largest Cuban-owned bank in the country, and invited me to fly to Santiago de Cuba with him and his son Fernando for the opening of that city's first branch office.

As a nineteen-year-old, I was fascinated with the business lesson I was receiving, although I could not comprehend the full magnitude of what he was telling me. Finally, thanks to his exceptional talent, Julián succeeded in bringing to fruition his idea of creating an empire in the national banking industry—after establishing branches all over the country, founding the Continental Bank, and making himself one of the most successful businessmen in Cuba.

When he found out that I was studying at the School of Agricultural and Sugar Engineering, he told me, "Come see me when you graduate—I'll have a job for you." That offer would be the seed from which would sprout a beautiful career in the sugar industry.

It must have been at the end of the summer when my job with the Zulueta family ended, and Brother Feliz called me with a job offer as a first-grade teacher for the next school year. It seems that Julián Zulueta had spoken well of me and my work with his sons, and I accepted the job immediately. The $75-a-month salary mattered little—it was a beautiful experience that I remember with great affection. I learned many things from Brother Feliz, a great educator, and truly enjoyed teaching seven-year-olds, whose minds are so receptive to all the new things we show them. I suppose that everything I experienced at Belén became very useful when I was educating my own children, as well as when I taught them to play chess.

While I waited for the classes to begin in September, I took a job working for a friend from Havana University as a public-opinion survey taker. The survey questions had to do with the forthcoming election, where Carlos Prío Socarras was eventually elected. I was paid $0.25 for each survey I completed. Being honest, whenever a household declined to participate, I did not report them, nor did I charge my friend for the attempt. Later, she found this out and told me that not only should I have been paid for those attempts but also that she was flabbergasted that I had not had any refusals. My honesty cost me a lot of quarters that summer!

Belén Jesuit School, Class of 1948—First grade, with their teachers Brother Feliz (far left) and me (tallest one in the back row). This was one of my first jobs in Havana.

The family is reunited

My family was finally able to be almost fully reunited in 1948, when my mother joined us in her native Cuba. The only missing piece of the puzzle was my sister Mela, but after getting married, she continued to live in Spain, moving between Madrid, the Canary Islands, and Barcelona. It was unbelievably wonderful to be together with our mother again, without the constant uncertainty of what could be happening thousands of miles away.

I was working nine to five in Belén School, driving to give private lessons to a student from 5:30 to 6:30, seeing another private student at 6:45, and then finally going home for dinner. I was still trying to complete my engineering studies but just did not have the time. After two years as a first-grade teacher, I realized that I was making more money giving private lessons, and I knew I could get a few more students, so I quit my job at Belén. I finally had the time and money to complete my university studies.

Our time together as a family lasted only four years: Everything changed when my father, always on the lookout for new opportunities, traveled to Toronto in 1952, to attend an international trade fair. There he met up with Albert Mevi, his old apprentice from the AEG company of Madrid. Mevi had become a successful businessman in the United States and, knowing my father's potential, offered him a job as a manager in his company to open the market in Madrid, Spain. The job required several months of training in New York, so my father moved there, accompanied by my sister Ana Maria. A few months later, they briefly returned to Cuba to pack their bags, and then, along with my mother, returned to Madrid.

Meanwhile, my brother Roberto and I were still in Cuba, and just about to graduate from the University of Havana (Roberto as a medical doctor, and I as an engineer), so we decided to stay in Cuba, believing that this would be our final destination. How wrong we were.

Back to the boards

Chess found me quickly during my time in Havana. After only six weeks on the island, I had received an invitation to participate in the Adler Memorial Tournament, along with some of the best players on the island. Of course, I accepted. My chess preparation in Spain was recent, and I was curious to know if I could compete as an equal with the most outstanding Cuban players, just like I had in my native Spain.

I began to frequent the Capablanca Chess Club almost every night. I played games until sleep won out, or until I considered it a reasonable time to rest, which is how I came to be known on the Havana chess scene. I met the most prominent players in the city, who would all come to the club, and my results were good enough to earn me an invitation to the Adler Memorial.

The Adler Memorial Tournament began marvelously; after four rounds, I was in the lead with 3.5 points, having defeated two of the most challenging opponents, Florido and Palacios. Unfortunately, the happiness lasted only twenty-four hours. The next morning, I received word that as part of my tutoring job with the Zulueta family, I had to leave Havana immediately to accompany them for two weeks on a trip that they needed to make. The children's education could not be interrupted, for any reason.

It was a frustrating situation that occurred at the worst moment, but it was even worse when I returned to Havana twenty days later. The newspaper reports of the tournament mentioned that I had finished at the bottom of the standings, without a single reference to the fact that I had withdrawn, giving the impression that I had played poorly.

After this first sad experience of having to withdraw when I was leading, I did not even try again for the next four years since I also had barely any free time. In January of 1952, the Cuban Chess Federation organized a national tournament to select the Cuban team to send to the upcoming Chess Olympiad in Helsinki. In Havana, they knew my history of tournaments in Spain, which is why I was invited to this important event. There were six available places for the Olympiad, and, despite facing fierce competition from top Cuban players such as Rogelio Ortega, Eldis Cobo, Eleazar Jiménez, Gilberto García, and the 1939 Olympiad team who had accompanied Jose Capablanca to the 1939 Olympics in Buenos Aires (María Teresa Mora, Miguel Alemán, Alberto López, and José Planas), I managed to finish in sixth place. I had earned a seat to participate in the Helsinki Chess Olympiad, where I would share a board with the strongest players on the planet! Furthermore, I had proved to myself that I could be competitive in Cuban chess.

However, everything crumbled with painful speed. The captain of the national team, Alberto Garcia, met with me to explore the idea that the sixth-, seventh-, and eighth-place finishers would play a small tournament to decide who would be the sixth member of the Cuban

Chapter 4: A New Life in Cuba

team. To convince me, he said that the three players would start with the points we had obtained in the tournament. I suppose they viewed me as a new arrival who was not even Cuban and had no chess credentials, while Rogelio Ortega and Gilberto García (seventh- and eighth-place finishers) had the highest credentials in Cuban chess. I felt it was unfair—what they offered me wasn't right. I had successfully defeated both players, and I was sure I could do it again, but why should I have to? They were trying to take from me what was rightfully mine.

And in that moment, like an echo from the past, Alekhine's advice came to my aid. My life was in full swing—working, completing my engineering studies, and starting to try and find a job in the industry for when I graduated. Alekhine was absolutely right—there are more important things in life than chess. So, although I thought it was incredibly unfair, I decided that I would concentrate on my career and forget about chess. I decided not to participate in the Olympiad and withdrew my name from further consideration. Ultimately, the seat on the Cuban team was filled by I.M. Rogelio Ortega, who had finished seventh. It was a blessing in disguise, and I truly learned how right Alekhine was. There is more, much more, to life than just concentrating on a single passion.

Still, in November of that year, Colonel Bolaños of El Salvador invited the Capablanca Chess Club to visit El Salvador for a match against the players from Guatemala and El Salvador. He even sent a Salvadoran Air Force plane to fly us from Havana to San Salvador! I was among those selected to go, along with Cobo, Alemán, the Spanish master Rafael Saborido (whom I had run into many times at the club and who had recently arrived from Catalonia, Spain), and four other players. It was a pleasant experience, and I feel privileged to have been able to live it.

Several weeks later, I played the team championship of Havana with the *Cubanaleco* (another prominent chess club) team, and we won the title of Champions of Havana. Just like at the Maudes in Madrid, I played third board; on first board was Dr. Juan González, second was Dr. Broderman, on fourth was Rafael Baquedano, and on fifth was Canovaca. That success would be my farewell to chess for sixteen years.

An unexpected visitor—Arturo Pomar

Life can take many turns, and it drove me to Havana. It did the same thing to my old friend Arturo "Arturito" Pomar, bringing him there for a few weeks when he participated in the international tournament of 1952. Havana was one more stop on his tour of the United States, Canada, and South America, and suddenly, a friendship was born. When you are far from home, and you meet someone you knew years ago in your own country, even a previously casual friendship becomes a close one!

I first met Arturito Pomar, child prodigy and chess sensation of Spain, in Gijón, in 1944, reconnected with him at the Castile team championship in Madrid, in 1945, and we played again at the International Tournament of Gijón of 1947. Although we were not close friends, I believe that the respect and good feeling between us was mutual.

During his days in Havana, we spent a good amount of time together. I took him around the city, and he asked to borrow my car so he could explore the city at night on his own. When you are young, you do crazy things—I lent him my car without a second thought.

Me with my beautiful car, the one that Arturito proudly drove around Havana.

In order to appreciate the full magnitude of why this was a questionable idea, you must understand a bit about driving in noisy Havana, where the only traffic law that was respected was the volume of your car horn. It is a city that has become an automobile museum, with thousands of cars from that era still circulating the streets. Those of us who learned to drive in Havana could drive anywhere, from Madrid to Rome to San Juan to Mexico City.

After teaching him the basics of "crazy Havana driving," including trips to the Malecón, San Lazaro, the university, and all of Route 23 until it crosses the Rio Almendares, Arturo felt prepared for the adventure. I also took him to visit the famous Belén Jesuit school, where I had been a first-grade teacher while studying at the university.

L-R: Pomar, Father Ceferino Ruiz (Rector of Belén School), and myself

Román Torán was also participating in the tournament. (In fact, he and Pomar ultimately shared eighth place.) Torán was one of the most active Spanish players at the international level at that time but was mostly participating in tournaments outside of Spain. He had just finished playing in a tournament in Punta del Este (Uruguay) and had written to the organizer of the Havana tournament, Alberto Garcia, expressing his interest in participating in the tournament and giving my name as a reference. I spoke of Torán in the highest regard, and they invited him to play. I also spent some time with Torán during the tournament; always restless and outgoing, he introduced me to a group of girls he had met at the beach who invited me to a party. I accepted and showed up there that evening. Although Torán never appeared, it did not matter—being single and unattached, I had a great time.

During the tournament, an incident occurred that clearly showed Pomar's personality. Torán and Pomar were staying at the same hotel during the competition, and they woke on March 10, 1952, to the notice that Fulgencio Batista (former president of Cuba), had staged a *coup d'état* against the current president, Carlos Prío. Torán, who listened to the radio every morning, heard the troubling news and went immediately to Pomar's room to tell him what had happened.

Pomar reacted surprisingly calmly, saying, "I heard, but I have a very difficult game this afternoon," and continued to shave as if nothing had happened. Torán, puzzled by his friend's calm, shrugged, and returned to his room. In spite of the tense situation, he was able to play in the tournament without a problem.

Another friendship left behind: Pablo Morán

One of the most positive aspects of chess is the friendships that spring up around it, and I have been very fortunate to count Pablo "Pablito" Morán as one of my best friends, in chess and in life. Anyone who knows the history of Spanish chess knows about Pablo Morán—he has written a multitude of interesting books about chess and is a true giant of Spain's chess journalism. Pablito Morán and I were neighbors in Gijón in the early 1940s, and we became friends then—a true friendship that lasted for life. We felt a strong bond at sharing the same life philosophy and, of course, chess. There were many afternoons and evenings when we took long walks along Begoña Park, discussing chess and life. Pablito was always a man of deep thought and sensitive nature, which was hidden behind his wonderful sense of humor and a cheerful personality.

Curiously, Pablo moved from Gijón to Madrid just when I left Spain for Cuba. His aunt and uncle had invited him to move to Madrid with them, hoping to give him a future with more opportunities than what he would have in Gijón. I mentioned the possibility of getting together at the Maudes club before I left for Cuba, which he accepted. There, I passed the baton to him—he took my place on the team while I packed my bags to start a new life.

Over the years, despite the distance that separated us, we stayed in contact. He kept me informed about our mutual friends and the chess life in Spain. In the 1960s and '70s, we got together several times, accompanied by our wives, Elena and Beatrice. We shared dinners at the *Club de Regatas* or spent unforgettable weekends with Pablo and his wife, Elena, at their beautiful vacation spot on the beach in Estaño.

Chapter 4: A New Life in Cuba

Photo that Pablo Morán sent me in 1951

Each time we were together, Pablo gave me one of his books with a dedication to me (which was not strange, given the considerable number of books he had written). I fondly remember his amusing dedications; in 1984, we went to Madrid, and he gifted me his book about Kasparov, with a dedication that reads: *"To my dear 'forever' friend, Eugene Salomon, citizen of the world and more Asturian than fabada* [a traditional Asturian dish] *as a memory of a meeting in Madrid after 37 years."* On another occasion, he gifted me the book he wrote about Bobby Fischer's life and games *with* this dedication, *"To Eugene Salomon, a friend like no other…as an acknowledgement for all your help in writing this book."*

It was with a heart full of emotion and fond memories that I dedicated my very first article in the quarterly newsletter of the *Chess Journalists of America* to Pablo. I also want to dedicate to him the award it won: "Best Personal Narrative (Online Article)." It seems appropriate—a chess journalist magazine honoring a giant of chess journalism!

CHAPTER 5:
Making My Way
(1953–1960)

My understanding of "the 1950s" in the United States brings to mind thoughts of Elvis and black-and-white TVs, but it was a very politically and scientifically active decade as well. The world was still recovering from World War II and the Korean War, communism was a major issue, and the "space race" had begun. My life in Cuba during the '50s was exciting as well as challenging, and those global concerns would soon affect me personally.

When I left Spain, I could not possibly have imagined the multitude of human experiences I would have in Cuba. Some were sad, but most were surprisingly beautiful. As pleasant as chess was, that was far from my only passion—I also derived a great deal of satisfaction from my business life. In Cuba, it took a grueling five years to complete my two degrees in agricultural engineering and sugar technology while having to work long hours at the same time.

Chess is my oldest passion and can be traced back to Gijón 1941, continuing in Madrid, Havana, and New York—four beautiful locations. However, my main passion (and secret of my success) is my work in the field of sugar and edible molasses, which was born in Havana and took me all over the world. My memory easily flies back to many trips and allows me to reminisce about those bygone days in London, Santo Domingo, Barbados, New Orleans, Montreal, Caracas, Puerto Cabello (Venezuela), Rio de Janeiro, Maceió (Brazil),

Frankfurt, Zurich, and Córdoba, all related to sugar specialty products including Edible Molasses.

A brief introduction to the world of sugar and edible molasses

The sugar industry is fascinating in many respects. You may not be aware, but sugar can be made from either sugarcane plants or sugar beets. Sugarcane grows only in tropical and subtropical areas, but sugar beets can be grown in temperate zones. While the first attempts at sugar beet processing did not occur until the mid-1700s, sugarcane processing history dates back to India around 4000 BC, and the resulting sugar was very expensive before the days of Columbus.

Columbus' "discovery" of the tropical Caribbean islands yielded an ideal place to develop sources of supply. It started with "Hispaniola" (the Dominican Republic) in 1501 and continued with many sugar mills in Cuba and Jamaica by 1520, followed by Brazil. By 1540, there were some eight hundred small cane sugar mills in Northern Brazil. It was also the beginning of a new phase of technological developments in sugar processing, which were further enhanced by the Industrial Revolution in the coming centuries. At one time, Haiti was a major player in global sugar production, but its sugar industry collapsed during the Haitian Revolution (1791–1804). Many of Haiti's planters and sugar experts fled the war and settled in Cuba and Louisiana, enabling sugar producers in both places to take advantage of the demand for sugar created by the loss of Haiti as a top supplier.

In 1812, Louisiana became a US state and was the main sugar supplier to the US, although Cuba was also supplying sugar, molasses, and rum to the US. Cuba's sugar connection to the US continued, and by the late 1800s, Cuba was exporting about 80 percent of their sugar to the US.

In my days, Cuba was the major worldwide producer of raw sugar from sugarcane. The cut sugarcane from thousands and thousands of acres of land was transported by rail and/or trucks to the "*central*" (sugar mill) where grinding extracted the juice from the cane. This juice, after being processed via filtration and sedimentation, ends up as a clarified juice that must be concentrated via evaporation to the consistency of a syrup. This concentration process is conducted in a "Multiple-Effect Evaporator" that operates under vacuum.

After that, the syrup is further evaporated until it crystallizes, so that the sugar crystals can be separated (by centrifugation) from the *molasses*—the syrupy product left after the crystallized sugar is removed. Typically, the process of crystallization and centrifugation is repeated two to four times, extracting more sugar each time, so that each successive molasses contains more minerals and less sugar. At some point, the balance of sugar and mineral content makes it economically unfeasible to continue the process of crystallization/centrifugation. The "final molasses" (also called blackstrap molasses) then goes into large storage tanks for distribution to the animal feed industry or to alcohol or rum distilleries.

Due to its high mineral content, blackstrap/final molasses has always had a good reputation for its health/nutritional value. When I was the head of a sugar mill in the province of Havana, we sold part of our final molasses to the Arechabala Distillery for use in the production of rum. The molasses was transported by rail in tank cars. I remember with a chuckle that around 1957, there was a widespread belief that blackstrap molasses had an aphrodisiac value—and the word spread as fast as the wind. You can imagine what happened—a revolution in progress! It became so acute that our tank cars, whenever they had to stop in any intermediate station, would be vandalized. People would climb on the tank cars and fill their containers with our molasses. We were forced to seal all the openings of the tank cars to avoid problems.

Edible molasses (also called cane juice molasses or CJM) is a specially manufactured sweetener and a completely different item. It is a product manufactured from the cane sugar juice, but without any crystallization—only processing and evaporation. (In order to avoid the crystallization, the sugar content is hydrolyzed, either with phosphoric acid or yeast so that the sucrose is partly converted into dextrose and fructose to avoid crystallization.) This product, known in the industry as "edible molasses," is such a specialized field, such a niche market within the sugar industry, that very few people even know about it. Consequently, I became what some people refer to as "the foremost authority in the world" in this field. Of all the sugar factories operating in Cuba, only one, *Central Providencia* (the one that I managed), produced edible molasses that was exported into the US outside the quotas limiting the importation of sugar.

My first sugar job—*Central Fe*

When I graduated in 1953, Julián Zulueta, as he had promised during my time tutoring his sons, offered me a most challenging position at his sugar mill, *Central Fe,* in Camajuani in the historic province of Las Villas. (The Spanish word *"central"* is widely accepted as referring to a sugar mill.)

My main position was chief chemist, and at the same time, I was given the responsibility of agricultural manager of his Colonia San Benigno (some 430 acres of cane fields). As agricultural manager, the first step was to create a blueprint of the farm's cane fields, which would be my first (and last) job in surveying. I have always been very proud of that, my first job, which is why I must include it in this book. (I also still have my original drawing.)

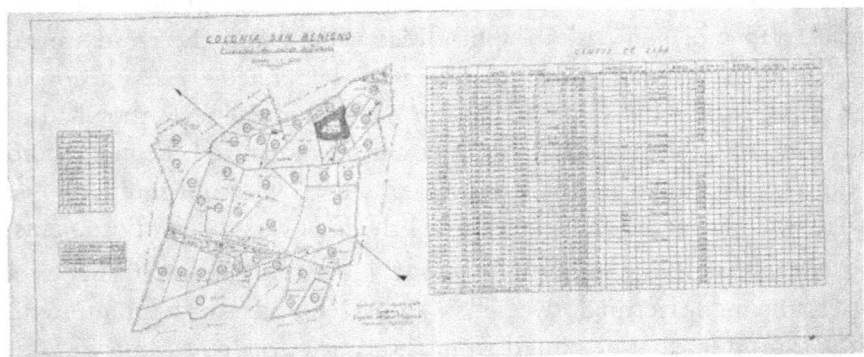

Blueprint of the San Benigno sugar cane farm, hand-drawn in 1954 for one of my first professional jobs.

The figures on the right are the results that I was obtaining of the yield of the cane planted in those areas under different conditions. It was a lot of work, and I am still very proud of it.

It was a hell of an entry point into the sugar industry for a recently graduated young man. I converted that farm into a center of agricultural experimentation, evaluating the effect of pre-heating the "cane seed" (actually small pieces of cane) on water at 52 degrees centigrade for twenty minutes before planting. (This was like a follow-up of a test run in Louisiana earlier as a prevention for the cane stunting disease.) While I never published the results of my findings, something quite interesting happened in the process.

I had read somewhere that although the Louisiana experiment was primarily for the prevention of stunting disease, the results had shown an acceleration in start-up growth and an increase in tonnage. The researchers thought that it was all due to the inversion of some sucrose into dextrose and levulose, accelerating the growth. I still remember quite clearly that I thought, *Well, if that is true, why don't we add some invert liquid sugar to the heating water to further accelerate the growth process?* So, that is what I did—I added some "High Test Molasses" to the water that I had prepared in the laboratory, with a 75 percent "invert sugars" content. My thinking was that since the monosaccharides were the direct source for the small cane pieces to grow, having these additional sugars available had to be helpful.

Bottom line? Seventy years later, I still believe that it worked! I have no scientific proof, just my observation about how fast the rows I planted with the treated seeds germinated. It was a wonderful experience, full of learning and generating true passion for the industry.

Speaking of research, it is how I learned that rats, like humans, love the flavor of sweet orange. When I got the job at *Central Fe*, being single, they accommodated me in a room with a separate entrance, attached to the main owner's home. One night, after putting an orange Life Savers candy in my mouth, I went to sleep. The next morning, my right thumb and the wall near my head were bloody. I went immediately to the doctor, who said, "I do not know if it is a mouse or a rat… No, no—it is a rat." Apparently, while building the entrance to my apartment, they had not properly sealed all the holes, and a wise rat had found its way into my bed and enjoyed the orange flavor still on my fingers. Today, it is funny—at the time, it was a nightmare.

In August of 1954, after seven years of grueling work and study in Cuba, I was able to travel back to Spain to see my parents. (They had been with us until 1952, and then my father took a job that sent him back to Spain.) I was planning this trip while drawing the map of San Benigno. When I told my boss, Julian Zulueta, about the trip, he said, "You're not going before you finish the map, are you?" I had to work like hell for the next few weeks, but then I was finally able to spend a couple of weeks enjoying time with my parents and family all over Spain.

The end of another stage

Those were years of hard work and absolute dedication, and an unforgettable experience that allowed me to grow both professionally and personally. I will always remember the difficulty of driving through those sugar cane fields. Whenever I tell someone that driving in the snow reminds me of San Benigno, they look at me like I am crazy, but the explanation is simple. Driving a jeep through the muddy sugarcane fields is very similar to driving in the snow in Brooklyn.

However, there was one thing that was less than wonderful: I was a city boy. I had not even finished acclimating to living in the country, and on top of that, it was a real pain in the neck to drive four hours every weekend from Camajuaní back to Havana to see my friends. Although I admire the nobility of the *guajiro* (the noble Cuban farm workers who sometimes worked for a dollar a day and didn't think twice about sharing their *café criollo,* whenever I stopped at *el batey,* their housing settlement), I could not even think about the idea of spending the rest of my life in the countryside.

For that reason, I began to look for other work, closer to Havana. Together, with Manuel "Manolito" Hernández Fumero, my close friend who was pursuing a similar career, we bought a small, fifty-two-acre farm in La Salud, near Havana, with the idea of producing red cabbage. Since the farm would not generate enough income for my living expenses, it soon became clear that I needed a new job, and chess came to the rescue.

A game of blindfold chess that changed my life

I had been away from chess for several years. Those days, I played only friendly games, and almost always blindfolded, a format that impressed fans very much but was not terribly challenging for an experienced player. Manuel "Manolo" Suárez Carreño (an engineer friend of my brother and an important man in the sugar industry), knew of my love for playing blindfolded and invited me to play a game with him at his home. We arranged a date, and off I went. I think that he wanted to check whether my reputation was deserved or not. He had been a good player in his youth, so this task was not easy, but I ultimately came away with the victory. Thanks to that game, a good friendship was born between us.

Manolo knew that I wanted to return to living in Havana, and for that, I needed a job. One year later, he informed me that his friend, Manuel Aspuru, was looking for a "plant superintendent." With Manolo's letter of recommendation in my pocket, I went to meet Don Manuel Aspuru and got the job.

That is how, thanks to a game of blindfolded chess, I began working at *Central Providencia*, in Güines, some fifty km from Havana. It was truly a stroke of luck—Providencia was the only Cuban factory that produced edible molasses for the Sucrest Corporation, a connection that would be very important for me in the future.

At Providencia, I learned the importance of converting a commodity product—raw sugar—into value-added specialty products such as turbinado sugar for Kellogg's (the Battle Creek, Michigan, cereals giant) and edible molasses (also called CJM—cane juice molasses). Cane sugar edible molasses, a little-known specialty product, had a large market in the United States and Canada.

At *Central Providencia*, besides being plant manager, I was also in charge of service and maintenance of the agricultural equipment.

As I learned from his son-in-law, "Don Manuel" (as I used to call him with respect and admiration) had been quite impressed with my recommendations in the report: "*Hacia un rendimiento de 14 en el Central Providencia*" (Toward a 14 Percent Yield at Providencia Sugar Mill). and had passed it to him. (One of my recommendations involved installing sprinklers at each of the railroad loading spots to reduce the effect of the hot tropical sun on the cane while it waited to be shipped.)

Sometimes, you do not know what destiny will hand you, nor what events will affect your life. In this case, everything revolved around a chessboard that I could neither see nor touch.

University professor

Toward the end of the 1950s, there was an opening for an associate professor of rural industries (with emphasis on food technology) at the School of Agricultural and Sugar Engineers. I was the selected applicant and returned to the classroom after many years, but this time, there were university students in front of me instead of first graders.

It was late in the 1950s. I had daily contact with the workers in the sugar factory and on my own farm, as well as with the suffering *guajiros* in the sugar cane fields. Those experiences, combined with experiencing the rebellion and idealistic student movement up close at the university, helped me to understand the Cuban Revolution more clearly. It was an event that, like the Spanish Civil War thirteen years earlier, would dramatically change my life.

At that time, I had invited my parents, who had been so happy in Cuba years before, to return to Havana from Spain. They accepted, and I rented a furnished house in the *Reparto Sevillano* section of Havana. I spent weekends with them and occasionally other days since my house at the sugar mill in Güines was not far from theirs.

Left: Roberto's wedding to Chicha, circa 1952 in Havana. **Right:** My father, Roberto's wife, Conchita, my brother Roberto, and my mother, with Cristina and Robertín. (Chalet de Goicuria 809-Reparto El Sevillano, Havana, circa 1957–8)

More war

The March 10 *coup* that occurred during the 1952 International Chess Tournament in Havana established a military dictatorship led by General Fulgencio Batista and circumvented the elections scheduled for June. His dictatorship lasted for seven years. However, beginning on July 26, 1953, revolutionary forces led by young lawyer Fidel Castro began trying to overthrow Batista's government via demonstrations and student riots. Batista responded with media censorship and violence. After years of resistance and guerrilla warfare from revolutionaries, Batista's forces were finally defeated on New Year's Day, 1959. I still remember watching Fidel Castro's triumphal entry into Havana on TV—the same Fidel Castro I had met on my arrival in Havana twelve years earlier. The revolution had triumphed, and people's enthusiasm was enormous—they were full of hope for the future, and there was an overall good feeling at being liberated from General Batista.

Nevertheless, a year and a half later, on July 18, 1960 (already an unlucky day for me on which, so many years earlier, I had awoken to the reality of the Spanish Civil War), my personal situation took a sudden, sharp turn. That day, Fidel Castro appeared on TV giving a speech in which he remarked that it did not matter if you were a good professor; the important thing was to be a good revolutionary. For that reason, he continued, he was dismissing the provost and all the deans of the various faculties of Havana University. It was clearly a way to start controlling the narrative and eliminating the influence of any democratically oriented leaders.

I immediately understood that Cuba was not going to be a place where I could have freedom and develop my career. The next day, I sadly went to the university, but this time it was not to deliver a lecture. During the staff meeting with the rest of the faculty, I handed in my written resignation. It was clear that I needed to leave the country.

And so, once again, I prepared to face another trip in search of a new destiny, again leaving everything behind for a change of (hopefully refreshing) scenery. I desperately hoped this would be the last time I would have to face this situation. After Castro's television address, my decision to leave Cuba was firm—I was concerned about my parents' situation. They had returned to Cuba to enjoy a peaceful retirement, and they were not going to find it in such a tumultuous environment. (Castro's popular support was exceedingly high since Batista was the product of a military coup that had overthrown the democratically elected government of Carlos Prio in 1952.) By the middle of 1960, it became obvious to me that we had to leave.

Chapter 5: Making My Way

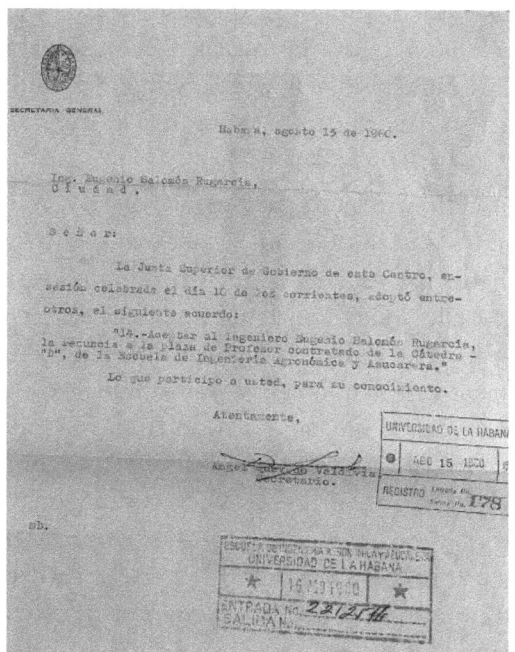

Letter from the University of Havana acknowledging receipt and accepting my resignation from my teaching duties.

Trying to get an exit permit

When we decided to leave Cuba, my parents did not encounter any legal hurdles when arranging their return to Madrid…but I did. When I tried to buy the plane ticket to the United States, the travel agency informed me that my passport had been retained, and I would need to go to the police station in person to claim it. I had no choice. To get it back, I had to put up with the aggressive and truly insulting attitude of a young captain who informed me, "You cannot leave the country. The Revolution needs all people with technical training." He did, however, offer an alternative—I could get an authorization to travel from the headquarters of the sugar industry.

These were dangerous times—accusations of belonging to the counterrevolution were commonplace, so I always took precautions. Whenever I spoke with the head of the union at the sugar mill, or with any other fervent revolutionary, I would nonchalantly mention the Spanish Civil War and my father's sufferings for being a left-wing liberal. I would conclude by showing my enthusiasm for the great heights that Cuban chess could reach, thanks to the growing friendship with the USSR. These strategies saved me from being blacklisted as a counterrevolutionary (later called *gusanos* "worms").

Unexpectedly, fortune smiled on me and gave me a way to obtain the exit visa. One of our clients was the famous American company Kellogg's, to whom we supplied thousands of bags of turbinado sugar every year. Six months earlier, Kellogg's had an agglomeration problem with the sugar that we had sent them. Manuel Aspuru, president and owner of the *Central Providencia* sugar mill, asked me to travel to the United States to see what was happening and to look for practical solutions. My English was technical and poor, but I always welcome a challenge and decided to travel to Battle Creek, Michigan, to investigate what was happening with our sugar. That trip was proof that I was not a flight risk, and my passport proved I had left and returned. This made it easier for me to obtain the authorization letter from the sugar industry—my only chance to obtain an exit permit, a required document that the Castro government had instituted in order to avoid the flight of technical people.

With these reasons in mind, I went to see a colleague and friend who oversaw the sugar industry in Havana. He was a political admirer of Castro but also a good friend. I explained that I had recently left for a visit to Kellogg's in the US and had returned promptly. Thankfully, I left with the desired letter of authorization in hand.

My eight years of professional career success, in Cuba, were, I believe, fair compensation for the hardships endured to complete my education. While working in the sugar industry, I got unique training about the ins and outs of the world of edible molasses and sugar specialty products. For a few years, I was in charge of the CJM (cane juice molasses) that a Cuban sugar mill produced for the American Molasses Company. Those work experiences and relationships were a great help in finding a job when life brought me to New York.

Chapter 5: Making My Way

Brothers reunited

Before leaving Cuba because of Castro, my father had the sad and deeply emotional experience of visiting his dying brother, Max, in Mexico. Due to Max's advanced illness, he was not able to verbally communicate with my father—the two were only able to shake hands. However, my father told me that by the feel of the handshake they shared, he could tell that his brother recognized him and was happy with their reunion after so many years apart.

Although my years in Spain had been very full of intense chess, my time in Cuba was not. Because of study and work, during the entire thirteen years I was in Cuba, I only had the opportunity of playing real chess during the year 1952. My first years in the US would continue that pattern.

CHAPTER 6:
The American Dream
(1960–1968)

Cuba was not going to be the place for my parents to enjoy a well-deserved retirement, nor for me to enjoy the airs of tolerance and human solidarity that I had learned from my father. It was time to leave. In early November of 1960, after having first arranged for my parents to board the *Marqués de Comillas* and return to Spain, I took a flight that brought me to the United States with the firm and unwavering idea of not returning to Cuba.

Thankfully, my situation was not as desperate as it might seem. I had friends in Miami, and my brother Roberto lived in Topeka, Kansas. He had left Havana with his wife, Conchita "Chicha," and their two small children in 1958, just before Castro, for a three-year training program in psychiatry at the famous Menninger Foundation. In addition, my father's first cousin, Frank Sanders, born Franz Salomon, who had fled Germany because of Hitler, resided in New York with his wife, Lola. I was also fortunate that Rudy Joseph (another of my father's first cousins who I had first met a few months earlier in Cuba) also lived in New York with his wife, Mildred. Very soon after my arrival in NY, I had the opportunity to visit both couples, and we have remained in close contact ever since.

This time I was traveling light…only a small bag (with my Alekhine chess pieces inside!). I was leaving behind a life built with effort and dedication. This trip was surrounded by even more uncertainty than the last one: I was traveling alone, no one would be meeting me in Miami, and I would be arriving in a country with vastly different customs and a language that I did not speak...with only five dollars in my pocket. I had no way of knowing that my eight years of professional experience in Cuba would wind up being incredibly valuable for my new life in the United States and be the reason for the meteoric trajectory of my management career in the US.

I flew from Havana to Miami, and I went to stay with my friend, Agricultural Engineer Eustaquio Ricondo (*el guajiro Ricondo*) who had been my boss at the *Central Providencia* sugar mill where he was the general manager. After a few days with him, I called Andy Jackson, head of Applied Sugar Laboratories, the R&D group of the American Molasses Company (which changed its corporate name to Sucrest Corporation one year later). Andy was the company's executive who had traveled to Cuba every year for the CJM production quality inspection and who had told me he would like to have me on his team if I ever left Cuba. Andy called me back, asking me to fly to New York for a job interview with Frank Staples, the company president. Ricondo lent me $300 and his overcoat, and I flew to New York.

I went with Andy Jackson to meet Frank Staples at the Sucrest corporate office: 120 Wall Street, at the bottom of Wall St. overlooking the river. The building was known in New York as "The Sugar Building." American Sugar Refining was on the sixteenth floor, American Molasses Company (later Sucrest Corporation) was on the nineteenth floor, and the Dyer sugar brokerage house, then directed by Dan Dyer, had their offices there as well.

The interview went well, and I was hired on the spot as a research chemist in a sugar refinery in Brooklyn, New York (where I fortunately did not need to speak too much). It was a wonderful opportunity: I could learn English and get an up-close look at the American business practices. My plan was to return to my native Spain with my family, with knowledge that would make it easier for me to find work there.

I had come to the US with a tourist visa. After the Cuban Revolution, Cubans were received with open arms in the US and were easily granted "green card" permits to live and work there. I had Cuban citizenship and was coming with a Cuban passport, so it should have been easy for me to get my green card. However, under the immigration quota system in place at that time, I was considered an immigrant from Spain (my country of birth)...and the Spanish quota had a waiting list of five years.

I realized that as a research chemist, I would need valid documents in order to work and travel and went to see Sucrest president, Frank Staples, a brilliant MIT engineer who solved the problem: "Effective today," he said, "you are no longer an employee but a consultant. We will only pay your travel expenses and keep the rest until our lawyers help you to get a work permit." As he directed, I went to see Stroock & Stroock & Lavan, the distinguished downtown law firm that had operated in NY since the late 1800s. The letter that a young lawyer, Schneider, prepared for immigration was so complimentary that, my God, you would think that the economy of the US would have collapsed without me!

As a result, I received a special letter from the immigration director granting me a temporary permit to work and travel until there was an opening in the "employment-based preference category" of the Spanish quota, a special priority designation for highly skilled people who wanted to enter the US.

American Molasses Company becomes Sucrest

As soon as I arrived in New York, I started working. Sucrest was the world leader in cane juice molasses in addition to operating two sugar refineries. The business also had a division dedicated to final molasses (blackstrap molasses) as livestock feed, a product they distributed via plants in Wilmington, Boston, Montreal, and Dartmouth.

Sucrest's most profitable product line was Edible Molasses (molasses for human consumption), which has its roots in the history of two families—the Taussig family in the United States, and the Crosby family in Canada. (In colonial times, the Taussig family ran a bakery in Washington DC, where they used edible molasses, a product that was even included in the provisions for George Washington's army.)

As I became responsible for Sucrest's molasses operations, I traveled to Barbados every year in February for the yearly purchasing negotiations with the Barbados Fancy Molasses Company, a main world producer of Edible Molasses. (Barbados' two major clients were Crosby Molasses in Canada and the Sucrest Corporation.) On one of my first trips to Bridgetown, Barbados, to negotiate the company's annual contract with Barbados, I met the Crosby family, owners of Crosby Molasses. That was one of many meetings with the Crosby family and one of many wonderful trips to Barbados.

Meeting the love of my life

Things rarely go as planned, and in the end, we are subject to what fate wants to make of us. A month after my arrival, I attended the Christmas party at the sugar company's headquarters (120 Wall Street). There, I met my future wife, Beatrice—a girl from Brooklyn, of Italian origin, who caught my attention. I could barely speak English (and was even worse on the dance floor), but I decided to ask her to dance anyway. She realized that I could not speak English and began to talk to me in a slow and musical Italian, just close enough to Spanish that we could communicate, and suddenly, we were having a conversation. The year 1961 was one of bilingual romance—I had an excellent reason to learn English fast! Bea, with a fluent Italian base, learned Spanish quickly—as "bilingual souls," I guess our communication was better than normal.

When life repeatedly shakes you, you learn to appreciate the good times. Since the day we met, the good times have always been with Beatrice (Bea) at my side. I remember many of them, but some occupy a favorite corner in my memory.

New York's famous Fifth Avenue begins in Washington Square Park, located in the heart of the New York University (NYU) campus. The park was a bohemian place, where the natural beauty of the location blended with the notes of the musicians who had gathered there since the 1940s. In 1961, the parks department commissioner, Newbold Morris, banned the playing of any kind of music there. The musicians, believing that this ban could not be serious, continued to go to the park...until the police came and forcefully arrested ten of them.

At that time, I used to go with Bea to Asti's, a restaurant four or five blocks from Washington Square Park and the nearby Marshall Chess Club. Bea had a true passion for music, and this restaurant was the right place to enjoy it since several of the waiters were professional opera singers who performed for the diners. Being so close to the park, we could never resist the temptation to go there and, despite the prohibition, sing to the music played by musicians rebelling against a senseless law. A large circular chorus formed, and we sang, while several people, stationed at the four corners, watched for the possible appearance of the police.

"Joe," a wonderful guitar player once featured in *The New York Times*, played his guitar artfully. At one point, he began to walk slowly through the circle of singers, looking for something...or someone. At last, he found what he was looking for: He stopped in front of us and, after ordering everyone to shut up, he asked Bea to be the one to accompany him vocally while he played his guitar. The sound of the guitar was delicious, but it paled in comparison to the magical voice of "my guardian angel." I think Bea's passion for music was what made her understand the intensity of my passion for chess.

My wedding and *Central Romana* (The beginning of my sixty-year sugar/molasses career in the US)

My first assignment, when Sucrest hired me in November of 1960, was to develop a new source of supply to replace Cuba. Since I had been in charge of edible molasses production at *Central Providencia* in Cuba during the 1950s, I was a logical choice.

As a first step, I visited several sugar mills in different countries. One of the countries was the Dominican Republic, as the owners of *Central Romana* had expressed an interest in the project. I traveled to Santo Domingo, capital of the Dominican Republic (while dictator Trujillo was still in power) for an exploratory visit. Without question, it was the ideal place!

Upon my return from Santo Domingo, we scheduled a meeting

with officers of the South Puerto Rico Sugar Company (owners of La Romana Sugar Mill in the Dominican Republic). It was still early in 1961 when Mr. Redman (manager of *Central Romana*) flew to New York for a meeting at our 120 Wall Street office. Mr. Debevoise, Mr. Spaeth (president and corporate VP of South Puerto Rico Sugar Company), and Mr. Redman (VP of *Central Romana*) met with Mr. Staples, Mr. Saufley (president and corporate VP of Sucrest), and me (a research chemist for Sucrest) for a serious negotiation regarding an exclusive production and purchasing agreement. That was the birth of a long-term contract that continued for thirty years!

Soon after crafting our agreement, there was a board meeting where concern was expressed about doing business in the Dominican Republic where a dictator (Trujillo) was in power. For a few weeks, I felt frustrated—after all our efforts, we were unable to go forward with the contract. To our shock and surprise, Trujillo was assassinated shortly thereafter, and the plan could finally be implemented.

I guess that it must have been September/October 1961, when, after a ten-month bilingual (Spanish-Italian) courtship, Beatrice and I decided to marry. We had booked the church (the Basilica of Regina Pacis in Brooklyn, a very well-known church) and the reception hall for December 9, a Sunday. Prior to making the arrangements, of course, I had cleared it with my boss (Harold Saufley) and had requested a week's vacation. Three or four weeks later, I got a phone call from Mr. Saufley that went like this:

"Gene, I was advised today that you have to be in *Central Romana* on December 10th."

"Mr. Saufley, perhaps you forgot that I'm getting married on December the 9th."

"Yes, I know."

My response: "Okay, let me see what I can do...."

So, that evening I went to see my sweetheart (then and now!) and presented the problem in the most favorable light possible. "If we can move the church and the reception to one week earlier, we can still go to Puerto Rico as planned for a few days' honeymoon, and then continue to Romana for a couple of months' extended 'working honeymoon.'"

Luckily, both the church and the reception hall were able to reschedule the dates!! There were some expenses (including having to reprint the invitations, etc.), but the company agreed to absorb all my extra costs. It was a beautiful solution (I thought) ...until I got a message from the president of the company, Mr. Frank Staples. He wanted to see me in his office...if possible, that afternoon at 2:00 p.m.

By then, I could speak English without difficulty, although I was still learning new words here and there. That afternoon, I learned a word that I will never forget: "paramount." As I sat in front of Frank Staples' desk, after a few brief questions came his message, "Gene, I want you to know that the production of CJM (cane juice molasses) is a project of "paramount" importance for our company...and therefore, I question the wisdom of your bringing your newlywed wife to the Dominican Republic until the operation is running smoothly and the quality of the product is guaranteed."

So, I went back to my bride-to-be to try to figure out a new solution for a new problem since she would not be able to accompany me. By sheer coincidence, my sister Ana Maria was teaching Spanish at a high school near the beautiful Blue Mountains of Jamaica called Clarendon College. I proposed this to Bea: "Let's stay in Puerto Rico for three days and then spend another three days in Kingston, Jamaica. Then I will leave you with my sister, and as soon as production is organized well, I will come and pick you up." She agreed, and we proceeded along these lines.

Finally, on December 3, 1961, Beatrice and I were married. My brother came from Topeka, Kansas, to be my best man. During the evening reception, the only people from my side were my brother and sister-in-law Robert and Chicha, and second cousins Frank (and wife Lola) and Rudy (and wife Mildred.) It was a small party—a total of only sixty people since most of my family was in Spain. The picture below reflects the deep love for Bea I felt then, and still feel to this day.

Sweet Memories — Family, Friends, Chess, and Sugar

After the wedding, on December 3, 1961, we honeymooned in Puerto Rico and Jamaica as we had planned. One day, before I was to fly to Santo Domingo to begin my work at *Central Romana,* my boss Harold Saufley phoned me (after he made me change all my plans), saying, "Gene, I was just advised that there is a strike at *Central Romana*, so you can extend your honeymoon, and I will advise you when to fly." I responded, "Sorry, Mr. Saufley, but my financial situation does not permit me to extend my vacation. As of tomorrow, I am working—what do you want me to do?" He said, "Okay, Gene, just try to organize visits to the sugar mills in Jamaica and write a report about it, while we wait for the strike to settle."

I had just visited a couple of Jamaican sugar mills when I got word that the strike had been settled. I flew from Kingston to the Punta Caucedo airport in Santo Domingo, where a *Central Romana* car picked me up for the drive to the mill. It was the first day of forty years of visiting *Central Romana* at least once a year in the 1960s, and more like four to five times per year in the 1990s in various, but always exciting, capacities. It was a rather unique experience!

This happened in December of 1961, and I have a broad smile when I relive it sixty-one years later! I had left Havana single, with $5 in my pocket, and here I was, one year later, taking my wife on a winter honeymoon in Puerto Rico, Jamaica, and the Dominican Republic… while still with only $5 in my pocket. (Maybe there was some truth to that line from the *West Side Story* song lyric in "America" that goes, "Everything free in America, for a small fee in America…")

These sweet memories of Santo Domingo combine the beginning of a sixty-one-year marriage, an equally long business career, and the birth of very meaningful friendships. Newly married and apart from my lovely bride, I never worked so hard in my life to organize production and improve the quality of edible molasses so fast! On the weekends, I would fly from Santo Domingo to Kingston, the capital of Jamaica, to visit Bea; she still kids me today that she spent her honeymoon with her sister-in-law. About ten days later, when we got production under control, I was able to have my wife by my side again. We began a two-month extended working honeymoon in the middle of winter in the Caribbean, on the property of the *Central Romana* sugar mill in the Dominican Republic. Life can be beautiful.

Mr. Redman (company VP) provided us with a small house bordering the ocean and next to the pool club, on the road where all the executives of the sugar mill had their homes—they were our new neighbors on the same road bordering the Caribbean. We became especially good friends with Pete and Camille Triviz, a young couple with two children. (Pete was the plant operations manager.) We even lent them our New York apartment and car for their stay in New York City to attend the World's Fair since we were away in Spain at the time. Our friendship continued in later years, when Pete oversaw production at one of the Louisiana sugar mills, and I visited them for many years on my business trips there. We also became close with the Redman family, another set of wonderful neighbors. On one of my trips to Madrid, we met up with the Redmans and did some sightseeing together.

I went from CJM (cane juice molasses) in Cuba to CJM in *Central Romana*, and went from being an avid player of social bridge in Havana to discovering the new amazing competitive game "duplicate bridge" in Romana. Duplicate bridge was so widely played among *Central Romana* executives that one might think it was a requirement for those in management positions! Those 1961–1962 honeymoon days were just the beginning of many new experiences and new friends.

My brother, Roberto

Unfortunately, after a few weeks, happiness was interrupted by tragedy: I received a phone message while working at *Central Romana* that my brother Roberto, in Kansas, had just been diagnosed with inoperable cancer. Roberto was especially important within my family—he had sacrificed everything to accompany my father into exile in 1943. In Havana, he had worked tirelessly, and his contribution was fundamental for reuniting the family in Cuba. He had completed his medical studies while working and yet still had time to volunteer with the Red Cross during the monstrous cyclone that devastated Havana in 1944.

As soon as Bea and I returned to the US from the Dominican Republic, I took a few days' vacation and flew to Kansas to visit my brother. It was a short and truly heartbreaking visit but was inspirational at the same time. On my second day there, Roberto asked me to accompany him on a few errands. Our first stop was at the bank, where my brother asked for the manager, and after introducing himself, he told him, "My home mortgage is with you. I have been diagnosed with cancer, which, as a doctor myself, I know will be terminal, and I want to leave everything in order for my family."

A couple of months later, when Roberto was coming to New York to the Sloan-Kettering Hospital in a desperate attempt to save himself, my parents came from Madrid to stay with him during the last few weeks of his life. They stayed with us in Brooklyn, and later on, I flew with them to Topeka, Kansas, for the last few days and his burial. (Sadly, Beatrice could not travel as she was expecting our first son.)

Those were days full of tragedy, mixed with inspirational moments. During my brother's last days, Dr. Karl Menninger himself came to my brother's bedside to personally present to him his diploma of graduation from his three-year psychiatry course at the Menninger Institute. Father Llorente, the director of the ACU flew from Miami for their last "Adios" from the church pulpit at the funeral.

Since their three children were so young, the family had decided it would be best to have the two older ones stay with friends during Roberto's final days to avoid their trauma. After Roberto passed, I needed to go pick them up in Osawatomie, Kansas, some ninety miles away. (Chris and Bobby were staying with dear friends from Cuba whose husband was a doctor at the hospital.) I will never forget the heartbreaking question from my five-year-old nephew: "Is Papa looking down on us from heaven now?" After Roberto's death, his wife, Chicha, and their children returned to Spain since her parents and mine resided there at that time.

A final note to my beloved brother: Wherever your spirit may be, I want to say thanks again for all you did to help our father to reunite the family and return to "normal family life" after twelve years of separations and undeserved hardships. Double thanks for your tremendous help to make my transition from Madrid to Havana as simple and pleasant as it was. Your life's example is always with me.

Chapter 6: The American Dream

My own family life begins

With this bittersweet mixture that is life, we returned to New York in 1962 and began to build the foundations of our family life. On a much happier note, our oldest son, Gene, was born that year. (I am pretty sure that Gene was conceived in Jamaica, so when he fell in love with Harry Belafonte and Jamaican music at age three, it seemed appropriate.)

I was focused on my career, and within two years, I was promoted to process research engineer for Sucrest's sugar refineries (New York and Chicago) and the molasses plants (Dartmouth and Montreal in Canada, and Boston, Wilmington, New Orleans, and Los Angeles in the US). At that time, Sucrest and its subsidiary, Colonial Molasses, were the dominant players in Louisiana's molasses industry. The original owner of Colonial Molasses, Harold Saufley (by then a VP at the Sucrest Corporation), asked Arthur Evelyn, the legendary molasses broker who knew everyone in the industry, to introduce me to the (then) five Louisiana molasses producers. After that, I visited New Orleans regularly to purchase the edible molasses annually, as well as to visit Colonial Molasses' New Orleans plant.

In addition to my success with finding a new source of supply for CJM, I had also recommended (and succeeded in) changing the pricing formula of the contract between Sucrest and the South Puerto Rico Sugar Company (parent company of *Central Romana*) from "average of the world sugar and the American sugar prices" to the "world price" plus a small premium. That change had a bottom-line impact of hundreds of thousands of dollars of profit margin per year for Sucrest. However, since the entire Edible Molasses/CJM project was absolutely confidential, nobody knew the value of my contribution to the company.

As a result, I believe they wanted to promote me but without creating a conflict with other management personnel of higher seniority who were unaware of what I had been able to arrange. For that reason, a new position was created, Assistant to the President, and I was promoted to it.

As part of my promotion, I got a new office at the "Sugar Building"

(120 Wall Street) and got to know important industry leaders. As an obvious part of the training for a future executive position with the company, I became a frequent visitor for lunch at the sugar trade's favorite restaurant club, India House. Frank Staples, Dick Taussig (a Sucrest chairman of the board), or Harold Saufley would invite me to come along so that I could meet sugar leaders. It was a fascinating experience, and I got a true introduction to the "who's who" in the industry.

Off to London—for business and family

In 1963, after settling into my new office at 120 Wall Street (the nineteenth floor, overlooking the river), Mr. Staples sent me to the UK. He wanted me to further develop our technical cooperation with Tate & Lyle of London, an industry leader in specialty products from sugar. It was there that I learned about a special "fondant" (a very fine type of powdered sugar) for the candy industry, which our R&D team under Charlie Broeg would later develop under the trade name "Nulofond." (A few years later, we adapted it for pharmaceutical tableting purposes under the trade name "Nu-Tab.") At the time, Sucrest was the northeast US distributor of C&H's (California & Hawaiian sugar refinery in California) product, a baking fondant called "Drifond." Developing our own process for the candy fondant led to the successful negotiation of a cross-licensing agreement for both fondants, between Sucrest and C&H.

Another coincidental breakthrough from my first 1963 visit to Tate & Lyle was my initial contact with the blackstrap molasses leader of the world, "United Molasses," at the time a subsidiary of Tate & Lyle. This initial contact was cultivated over the years with follow-up visits to London and came to fruition twenty-plus years later when I became president of the Specialty Products group. I decided that we should divest from the blackstrap animal feed business (Deep Water Terminals in Wilmington, Boston, Montreal, Hamilton, and Dartmouth), so I contacted United Molasses, and we had a most successful divestiture. By sheer luck, we completed the transaction while the price of molasses was high just before a severe fall, and we sold thousands of tons of molasses in storage at our five terminals in one day near the top of the market!

It was during that trip to London that, at my father's suggestion, I established contact with his first cousin Hans Wolf, my Grossmama's nephew. Years later, that initial meeting and the continued family contact would reveal a tragic story from WWII Germany (details in Chapter 15). This was also the year when we had our second child, our daughter Maria.

1963: Christening of our daughter Maria

They were beautiful times of family peace, living in an apartment in Brooklyn in the beautiful "Scandinavian section" on Shore Road, overlooking the New York Harbor entrance. From our apartment, we watched the monumental Verrazano Bridge construction. (The Verrazano-Narrows Bridge has a central span of 4,260 feet and was the longest suspension bridge in the world from 1964, until it was surpassed by the Humber Bridge, built in the United Kingdom in 1981.)

Fortunately, my father's quest for family unity continued in New York. The location of our apartment allowed our young family to regularly visit the Joseph family, my father's first cousins, in Long Island, as well as his other New York cousin, Frank Sanders, and wife, Lola, on Cabrini Blvd, near the George Washington Bridge.

Chess slowly reappears

In 1964, after four years of demanding work, we were able to enjoy a beautiful vacation in Spain. First, we made a stop in Madrid to see my parents, and then we went to the scenic Canary Islands, where my sister Mela lived. This was my first visit to my family in Spain since I had moved to the US.

My parents in 1964, when I went to visit them in Madrid.

Madrid, 1964: Left: My parents, Bea, myself, our children Gene and Maria, Chicha and her children Christina, Roberto, and Ani, and my sister Ana Maria holding in her arms "Cousin Ani," the youngest daughter of my brother. My father's and my mother's wide smiles convey just how proud they were of their family. **Right:** L-R: Christina with Gene, Ani, Roberto ("Bobby") with baby Maria

The 1964 vacation, with my wife and our first two children (Gene, age two; and Maria, age one) was beautiful. Traveling with two little

Chapter 6: The American Dream

children on an eight-hour flight was quite an experience, but all the complications were an insignificant price to pay for a family reunion.

This trip was two years after brother Robert had died, and his widow, Chicha, and their three little children had moved back from Topeka to Madrid. Both sets of parents, Roberto's/mine and Chicha's, were living in Spain—hers in Galicia and Roberto's/mine in Madrid. After Madrid, we continued to the Canary Islands to visit my sister Mela. On those beautiful islands, chess reappeared in my life through the tiniest crack.

Mela's sons, my nephews, Antonio (Toni) and Roberto (Rober), knew how to play chess; in fact, Rober would soon become the school champion of the Canary Islands. Even though I no longer played, my love for chess remained intact, so I could not resist playing several games against them. (I must confess that they gave me more trouble than expected.) I later learned that my father had taught them to play when he returned from Havana in 1960, giving them a solid foundation.

Many years later, Rober came to Princeton University in New Jersey, having received one of the ten scholarships that Princeton annually awarded to foreign students, and earned his doctorate in mathematics. During the time I spent with Rober, chess re-emerged in an unusual way. Juan Carlos Peral was one of Rober's fellow students, and when he learned that I used to play blindfolded, he was skeptical, believing that you couldn't possibly play well without seeing the board. I told him that, of course, you could play well blindfolded, and that it wasn't even exceedingly difficult to do, and he replied: "That cannot be—it just can't be."

I countered with, "Well, let's play, then. Not only will I beat you, but I will beat Rober also."

It was the first time that I had played two blind games at the same time, and I wondered if I had gotten carried away and been too daring in my challenge. As Rober remembers this event: "While my friend Juan Carlos and I racked our brains, my uncle easily killed us, while also nonchalantly chit-chatting with the rest of the family there."

After the games, commenting on chess in general, Rober mentioned his experience as a young kid in Spain, and I asked him to write about it for this book. This account of Rober's chess experiences at his championships of the sixties is an interesting testimony and a small tribute to our first teacher, my father, and will hopefully demonstrate how deeply the love of chess is ingrained in our family.

A school champion from the distant Canary Islands (Excerpt)
By Roberto Moriyón

In my childhood, I was lucky to be in close contact with classical music and chess. My father, and my grandfather/godfather, Robert, had a passion for music like few others I have ever known. Thanks to them, music has been a refuge throughout my life and a source of incredible energy. Also, thanks to them, I have been able to enjoy chess, which undoubtedly played a significant role in my intellectual development (despite my limitations in considering the immense range of possible variants in each position on the board). During childhood, our grandfather gave my brother Antonio (fifteen months older than me and deaf) and me several chess books that we enjoyed for years, and which opened the doors of an exciting world to us.

Back then, my grandfather and my mother would tell us about our uncle Eugenio, who lived in Cuba (later in New Jersey) and was so good that he had almost made a draw playing simultaneous games with Alekhine when he was fourteen years old. I could not imagine that fifteen years later, it would be our connection when I arrived with my wife, Esperanza, in Princeton to do a doctorate in mathematics, and that he would soon become much more than just my uncle, thanks to the relationship we maintained for the next five years.

In the 1965–66 academic year, we lived in Las Palmas de Gran Canaria. The institute where we studied proposed that my brother and I should participate in the Canary Islands' school championship, in which the best players from each school would play. (I don't know that we were necessarily "the best"—I would say that we were the "least bad.") Antonio (Toni) played in the junior category, where the best players were, and I, having not reached the age of fifteen, played in the children's category.... Toni played four matches, mostly against boys who played well. He managed

Chapter 6: The American Dream

to get ahead and reach the finals, which he should have won easily since his opponent was not one of the strongest (fate had smiled on the pairings). Sadly, he fell ill with the flu, and his rival won the title of junior provincial champion.... For me, everything was easier, because I only had to play three qualifying rounds, plus the final match against a player who was still very green.

I reached the final match with a good chance of winning, thanks to the fact that my brother had done me the favor of getting rid of the strongest opponents, including himself, for which I was enormously grateful...and I won the title of Canary Islands school champion.

In June, I traveled to Madrid to participate in the national championship. My grandfather had the great idea of proposing that I stay at his house instead of the hotel where we were assigned. Even though the results in the tournament were not sensational, I have great memories of that week in which he and I shared joys, disappointments, and hours of analysis of the essentials of each day's games. These moments were precious, dedicated to him showing me positions that he considered worth knowing in advance because he thought that they might occur, or moves that were important to have prepared. I will always remember the bond that was created by working closely with someone who, aside from being my grandfather, had just become my friend.

There were more participants than I expected.... In my group, there were two players of a clearly lower level, but there was also the Madrid champion. In my game against him, I was lucky—we got to one of the situations that I had been preparing with my grandfather, which I played correctly, and beat him.

When I think about this whole curious adventure, more than fifty-five years ago...it was interesting and enriching, and the help of my grandfather (and namesake) was crucial. I am convinced that without him, I would not have managed to finish in as high a position as I did. But the most significant part of that adventure was how our relationship changed. My grandfather, even though in those years, distance was a great impediment to communication, became my confidant, someone I knew I could count on when I had to make problematic decisions or was overwhelmed by challenging situations. I felt immense pain when he died three years later while we were living in Barcelona. At that time, I was considering the possibility of studying mathematical sciences, as I finally happily decided to do—one of the most important decisions I have ever made.

Curiously, in my new great passion (bridge), I have found myself in situations comparable to the school championship of 1966. Most remarkable was my recent experience playing in the pairs category of the hearts championship in Gijón, Spain, in May of 2019. I again had the feeling that the most important thing was not having won a particular place in the standings, but rather, having been able to display, over the three days of competition, all the preparation and work that went into preparing for the tournament. I know that I am still just an amateur player, but I have no doubt that the experience that I have acquired in these years has increased my skill in the game of bridge. This is like what I gained while learning chess fifty or sixty years ago from my father and grandfather. That type of experience is most helpful in enhancing one's capacity to meet daily challenges at every stage of life, with the best chance of success.

From left to right: Toni with Maria Pía, my sister Mela, Rober, and Beatriz. Las Palmas 1964

Life goes on

Those Fridays of clams and beer after returning home from work in the Red Hook section of Brooklyn is a pleasant memory. Bea was waiting for me, watching for my car from the terrace, and we would drive to Sheepshead Bay for fresh clams and beer.

During the weekends, we were always busy, either with the group of our "bilingual friends" from Philadelphia (my old friends Javier

Chapter 6: The American Dream

Zulueta, Juan Jose de la Cierva, and Dr. Ernesto Bosch from Spain, among others) or with Bea's family, the Porcellis, who became my family as well. I fondly remember the "cousins club" we organized, with monthly get-togethers at various homes.

Traveling to Barbados: Truly a privilege

Sugar production in the tropics is always done in the winter when the sugar cane has its highest sucrose content. The edible molasses produced in Barbados used a different process from all the other countries, and the result was a special taste, making it one of the most desired products on the market. Traveling to Barbados from Canada or from New York in the month of February is a wonderful perk…and playing golf under the Barbados sun in the middle of winter is a rare privilege.

Sucrest always sent its president, Frank Staples, and executive vice president, Harold Saufley, to Barbados. In the mid-sixties, as part of my "training" as a future executive, Frank Staples decided that I would go to the annual contract negotiation in his place. I felt honored that the company selected me to travel to Barbados, where I had several interesting experiences, including dining with a member of the British royal family!

It was February, toward the end of the '70s, I believe, and we were traveling once again to Barbados. When we arrived, Harold Saufley remained at the hotel while I went to the city to buy some needed provisions for our stay. There, I ran into the Honorable Sir George de Lascelles, owner of one of the small sugar factories that produced Fancy Molasses, who quickly asked if Harold was in town. He immediately invited us to his home, as they were having dinner with his friends who had traveled with them from London. Harold was very happy to hear this and quickly accepted. After all, it is not every day one gets to dine with a member of the royal family—Sir George was a cousin of the Queen!

During dinner, the conversation turned to traveling, and Sir George's wife mentioned how expensive the transatlantic voyage from England was. Harold had taken a cruise to London several months earlier and was (I'm sure) prepared to offer his opinion on the matter,

105

but before he could speak, Sir George's wife added, "Yes, you must keep in mind that you have to hire crew members and, of course, a captain." She was referring to manning their one-hundred-foot yacht, whose silhouette we could see from the dining room of the house.

Understanding where this conversation was realistically headed, Harold commented, "I don't have that problem—because I don't own a yacht." Perhaps lacking comprehension of the differences between their situations, or having a good sense of humor, our hostess asked him, "Then what do you do with your money? Do you bank it?" A good laugh around the table ended the conversation.

1965—a very special year

The highlight of 1965 was without a doubt my drive to Brooklyn Court to become an American citizen. I had the additional privilege of having the last chairman of Sucrest, Richard S. Taussig, as my sponsor for my US citizenship ceremony. During the drive, from our home on Shore Road via the Belt Parkway, on my way to Borough Hall in downtown Brooklyn, I was thinking how incongruent that was with my family's history. Here I was, driving for my citizenship, and I could choose between Spanish citizenship (where I was born), Cuban citizenship (where I possessed a passport as a native citizen), and German citizenship (I was registered as a German citizen at birth, had it revoked by Hitler, so I had the right to recover it), and yet, I was about to elect to become a US citizen. I was mentally comparing that odd situation with the saga that my father had experienced forty to fifty years earlier, when he was stranded in France in WWII without any citizenship documents. He also faced citizenship decisions throughout his life: including after WWI, when he chose to remain German instead of becoming a French citizen when Alsace-Lorraine changed hands—a decision that cost them a family fortune.

How did I feel? I guess I was grateful, confused, overwhelmed, near tears…but smiling at the same time—sometimes strong emotions are difficult to describe. In a way, it was a reflection of what the Statue of Liberty stands for—and today, I will have to say, "*Thanks*" to a generous country for the opportunities, and for my wife and the four children and seven grandchildren who are my highest pride.

CHAPTER 7:
New Jersey, My Parents, and the NJ Open
(1966–1968)

The following year, 1966, Beatrice was pregnant and expecting "child number three" (as he calls himself). Henry was born in August, and shortly after that, while he was a baby, we moved to the suburbs, to our new home in Old Bridge, New Jersey. With three young children and a successful career, I had come a long way from not speaking the language in 1960 to being named corporate vice president of a New York-listed corporation in only six years.

1966 also brought another family vacation to Madrid, Spain, to visit my parents. That vacation was a chess memory extravaganza—it was the twentieth anniversary of my Maudes Chess Club team's first place victory at the Castile team chess championship. It would also be my last contact with my friend Arturito Pomar. Several months before the trip, I advised "Queima" (my great friend from the Maudes Chess Club) about my proposed vacation in Spain, and he immediately began to put together a program to celebrate with the old friends.

Since it had been twenty years since our victory, something special needed to be done. Queima called me a few days later to try to organize a small tournament in Madrid in which Arturito Pomar could participate since he was free on those dates. Pomar was happy about playing with us, but asked that the prizes be in cash, even if they were small, because otherwise, he couldn't play since he was a professional. I asked

Queima to thank Arturito in my name for the offer, but it had been more than ten years since I had played chess, and besides, I would be on a family vacation.

"Thanks, Queima, but forget about the tournament. We'll do a celebratory meal in tribute to our friendship." ...and that's how I lost the opportunity to play against Arturo Pomar again.

Family life in the suburbs

By 1967, with three children and a comfortable home, we began another kind of life—more relaxed, focused on raising our children in the healthy environment of the suburbs, where they had a lot of activities.

We now had a complete family (or so we thought), and we were adapting to New Jersey. Bea's mother (known and loved as the children's Italian grandma, *Nonna*) accepted our invitation to retire and leave Brooklyn to come live with us in New Jersey. That enriched our family life tremendously. The children won a second mother and a defense lawyer against a disciplinary father. Bea gained the freedom to accompany me and enjoy some of my frequent business traveling since we could, with eyes closed, leave the children with Nonna for occasional short trips. In addition, I got a very biased referee, always ready to settle any issue between me and her daughter...in my favor! From the very beginning, when Bea introduced me to her, Nonna adopted me as her son, and always took my side! Whenever we went on vacation to Europe, she accompanied us. I remember one summer when our oldest son, Gene, was about fifteen, Nonna took him with her to Bari, Italy, to spend a month with her family there. It was an incredible experience for our oldest son. Bea and I were happy with our new life, and our children loved the time with their grandmother, whom they adored. Nonna lived with us until her passing in 1979. She was an exceptional woman who we always remember with love.

Nothing is perfect in life, however. There was a price to pay—my daily commute was now at least 2.5 hours per day or more. Luckily, I was able to arrange the commuting situation quickly—I found four other nearby friends who were also working in the Wall Street business area. The carpool we organized worked very well for years.

Throughout the mid-sixties, my work life was just as full as my family life. I took all kinds of seminars (encouraged and paid for by the company) to supplement my foreign education, including several offered by the American Management Association, from "Finance and Accounting for Non-Financial Executives" to their most complete series of four weeks of general management. I also took a course at the Sugar & Coffee Exchange on "Commodities Trading" as well as a seminar on "Ship Chartering." These last two were very specialized and related to work for which I had responsibility.

With my arrival in New York, chess had disappeared completely from my life since an immigrant only has room for one thing in life—survival! Nevertheless, there was still a small gap where it was able to squeeze its way back into my life. On Sundays, when Bea and the children had something to do without me, I used to take the subway from Brooklyn to Manhattan to the famous Marshall Chess Club. This only happened once every few months, but it was an immense pleasure. Occasionally, the younger members of the club would play informal rapid elimination tournaments. I couldn't resist and asked if I could play—how surprised their faces were when I successfully defeated the rising star, Mark Lonoff.

By 1968, I thought my life had stabilized. I had a good, steady job, a lovely wife and family, and was living in a nice house in New Jersey. As we raised our children, memories of the abundant music of my childhood (with my wife, Bea's enthusiastic support) inspired a family rule that everyone had to take four years of piano as basic musical training. After that, they could continue any instrument they liked. Our oldest, Gene, took years of classical guitar and is a lawyer for some of the most famous musical current performers; Maria took voice lessons and later became a teacher, but still sings at benefit events; Henry continued to study and pursue piano throughout his life and is a keyboardist/vocalist in Houston; and our youngest, Robert, took his mandatory four years of piano.

The other "house rule" for our children was that they also had to be bilingual and could choose any language…as long as it was Spanish. Over the years, my children and grandchildren visited family in Spain frequently and even spent summers there, becoming close with their cousins, aunts, and uncles. Conversely, some of their children and grandchildren have spent time with us in the US. That was a great help in achieving my "bilingual dream"—my four children and several of my grandchildren are fluent in Spanish.

That year, 1968, I also became division president of a newly created division of the Sucrest Corporation while continuing as corporate vice president. Unfortunately, that year was also one of the saddest of my life—in the span of only six months, misfortune dealt me two terrible blows.

The loss of my parents

At the end of January 1968, I took the most painful flight of my life, the one I never wanted to take—I traveled from New York to Madrid to attend my father's funeral, arriving just in time to accompany him to the cemetery. It was a sad trip and a painful goodbye to the man who had been my inspiration in life and who had instilled in me not only his great love of chess and music but also his example of family love, human solidarity, and hard, honest work.

I remember how I received the news of his death: I had just arrived at my office, 120 Wall Street, and as I did every day, was gazing out from the nineteenth floor at the beautiful river and panorama in front of me, when my secretary informed me that I had a call from Madrid. I had a feeling it would not be good news, and it wasn't. My father had died of a massive heart attack. I closed the door, sat down, and cried tears of tender love that I never suspected I felt for him.

In Madrid, my friend Víctor García Queimadelos was by my side the whole time. It was fitting that at his farewell, my father, who loved chess so much, was mourned not by one but by two chess players.

Only six months later, tragedy made a return appearance in my life. My mother (that silent heroine who raised four children while her husband was far away) was suffering from painful end-stage pancreatic cancer. I decided to spend the last days of her life by her side, so I did not hesitate to put my family life and work on hold and rushed to Madrid. I went up to the fifth floor of the same Alonso Cano #3 apartment that I had departed twenty-one years earlier on my way to a new life in Cuba and accompanied my mother in her last steps through her life.

During those days with my mother, my old friend Queimadelos was with us again. He had visited my mother several times during her illness and was by our side during those difficult moments. We reminisced with my mother about the old days when, as high school students, we would meet there at my home.

They were bitter days, days of waiting...but everything comes, and everything goes in the incomprehensible adventure that is life, and the final moment for my mother finally arrived. I will never forget how I felt sitting at her bedside, just the two of us, as I held my mother's hand in both of mine. She trembled, and breathed her last breath, strong and resonant, in what would be her final goodbye. It was a life-altering moment for me, and I felt painfully alone as I thought, *Her spirit has gone to the unknowable and incomprehensible "great beyond."*

I had lost both parents in one year. I think that one's life changes drastically when their parents are gone—you really become solely responsible for your destiny without the comforting support of your parents. But life does not stop, and now I was the one who had to fight for my children, create bonds with them and protect them...in short, be a father.

Chess and the New Jersey Open

By 1968, my priorities (family and a business career) were developing very well. Could it be worth trying serious chess again at age forty? It didn't matter what country I found myself in, life always wound up pushing me far from chess...to which I always returned.

I'm not sure why, but after sixteen years of absence, I wanted to try once more, so I entered the 1968 New Jersey State Open Championship. My father had died several months earlier, but I believe that he gave me the necessary push to make the decision. His teachings (burned into my mind), his example, and his love for chess had always been with me, and in those days were more present than ever since he was no longer with us. My heart, not my mind, told me that it was his urging that pushed me to participate in this tournament.

I was once again seated before a chessboard, with that uneasy feeling that one has before a battle in a tournament. Seated across from me was my first opponent—Steve Pozarek, and I am certain that my father sat beside me throughout the entire game. Never before or since have I played a game with such intensity.

Curiously, Steve Pozarek's father was observing the entire game with great interest. He had been a strong player there in the 1930s and was responsible for having taught his son to play (there are too many parallels with my own life to ignore). I chatted with him after the game, trying to downplay my having defeated Steve, explaining that I had been a master in both Spain and Cuba.

Steve and I shared many moments after that, shaping a great and enduring friendship. Although it is not common for chess players to publicize their defeats, Steve published our game with commentary fifty years later, in a touching tribute to me and our friendship. I believe it might be interesting viewing what happened that day through Steve's eyes:

Gene Salomon, and the most important defeat of my chess career
By Steve Pozarek

In 1968, I was an eighteen-year-old chess player with an Expert rating (with ambitions of becoming a master). Just before the beginning of my second year in college, I entered the New Jersey Open. My opponent in the first round was unrated, which means that he had not participated in any qualifying tournaments (in the US!), and I figured he didn't have much experience in chess. I had no idea that the game would represent a fateful

Chapter 7: New Jersey, My Parents, and the NJ Open

moment for me, but, as I read recently, destiny doesn't have the reputation it does for simply doing what seems like it should happen.

In my youthful enthusiasm, I did not pay attention to the signs given by my opponent that he was not simply an ordinary unrated player. First of all, he was not a young child, he was a serious man of thirty or forty. Secondly, he was recording the moves not in standard US notation but in a language I did not know at all. Finally, he moved the pieces with the confidence of someone who had done it many, many times before.

Ignoring these warning signs, I made my first play, moving two squares my white pawn in front of the queen, something I had almost never done before that moment. When my opponent chose the King's Indian defense, I responded with the Sämisch Variation, a line that I had never played before (and have never played since!). After all, what could be the harm? He wasn't rated.

In movements 8 to 10, my opponent maneuvered his two knights in such a way that it seemed unusual to me. I believe that I saw it as more proof of his inexperience, but, in fact, it was a clear indication of my lack of understanding of the position. Very shortly afterward, I realized I was in trouble. Stunned by the sudden turn of events, I made several moves without a concrete purpose, while my opponent realigned his pieces with determination. On move 26, he had two pawns' advantage, and my position was collapsing on all fronts. In that moment, I resigned; it is probably the only time in my life where bowing my king represented a disappointment for the player on the other side of the board. My rival, "unrated" and without credentials, had calculated a beautiful checkmate in five moves that I didn't allow him to show in the game.

And that's how I met my lifelong friend, Gene Salomon! I was pouting after the game, and Gene consoled my father (who was also a very good chess player), telling him that although he was not rated in the United States, he had been a strong master in Spain and Cuba. The only reason why he didn't have a USCF rating was that he hadn't played any tournaments in the United States since his arrival ten years earlier. Actually, he hadn't played any tournaments in more than fifteen years.

For his performance in this tournament, Gene received a provisional USCF rating of master—a title it took me ten years to earn!

What would have happened if I had not been paired with Gene in that first round in 1968? Or, even more interesting (and tragic), what would have happened if the outcome of that game had been different? In hindsight, given the strength of Gene's game, it seems very unlikely that I could have won, or even drawn, that game. But if I had, would Gene have become discouraged and his results for the rest of the tournament been different? Would he have returned to his comfortable "chess retirement" to focus on his career and family? Who can know for certain? But yes, I lost that game! And given Gene's great success in chess during those years, together with his success in his family life and the business world, I believe that I can say with certainty that it was the most important defeat of my chess career!

Steve Pozarek with his father

A victory just out of reach

After the most encouraging first game, I was paired for the second one against a strong master, Steve Jones, who was curious about my having defeated a high expert in my first game. I thought that I owed him an explanation as to why I was unrated and gave him a briefing of my chess background in Spain and Cuba, so he was forewarned. I was able to beat him as well. After the fifth round, I led the classification with four points after having faced such strong opponents as Stephen Jones and George Kramer. (I had been well on the road to winning my game against Kramer, but one bad move destroyed all my prior work, and I had to concede a draw.)

In the penultimate round, I faced Mauricio Perea, a Spanish player who had become one of the strongest players in the state of Texas. It was not just another game—we were both playing to reach the final round, with the possibility of winning. But there was something else…something I couldn't put my finger on. Afterward, chatting with Mauricio, I discovered that our lives had been almost parallel roads, which gave us a connection that can only be understood by those who have shared the same tragedies and joys. Mauricio had also lost part of his childhood due to the Spanish Civil War and his emigration to Mexico. Just like me, he also developed a very successful business career (for him, in the pharmaceutical industry). He had come to the United States from Mexico as an executive in the pharmaceutical industry, arriving first in Texas, and later settling in the New York area.

Playing the game, we had no idea, nor did we even suspect, how closely our lives paralleled each other's. It was an equal fight, but I finally came up with the victory, which left my opponent with no way to reach the highest spots.

The last round came, and I had a serious chance of winning first place. Even a draw would win it for me—but it wasn't meant to be. In the United States, there was a practice I was unaware of—the final round is usually played on a different schedule. It is done earlier in order to give participants from other cities time to return to their homes. When I arrived at the tournament thinking I was arriving an hour early, I was actually an hour late. With that handicap, I could not play a normal game, and my opponent, Robert Wachtel, won the game and the title of champion. The defeat did not leave too bitter an aftertaste, though—it was a pleasure to prove to myself that I could hold my own against the best players not only in my native Gijón, but also in Madrid, Havana, and now, New Jersey!

CHAPTER 8:
The Foundations of a Life
(1969–1977)

They say that life begins at forty, and that is truly how it was for me. In 1968, I lost my parents, leaving me with a bitter void in my heart. However, I had also started a new chapter in my history: my own family, which was rapidly filling that void. There were years when my family and business gave me great satisfaction, converting adversity into success in a new country, following the example of so many immigrants, and with my father's inspiration always present.

In 1973, our last son, Robbie, was born. What an unexpected surprise! (I believe he was the result of a long business trip to Brazil.) Robbie's birth was indeed a beautiful happening and quite an experience for me, at age forty-five, to feel like a combination father and grandfather.

Although we now lived in New Jersey, whenever friends ask me about my children (three born in New York and one in New Jersey), I still say they are "typical New Yorkers": Their paternal grandfather was born in Metz, France (at that time, Germany); their paternal grandmother was born in Cárdenas, Cuba (really Spain at that time); and their maternal grandparents were born in Rutigliano, in the province of Bari, Italy. To complete the puzzle, their father was born in Spain, and their mother was born in Brooklyn. What a mixture! As I said, typical New Yorkers!

Climbing the ladder at work

The worlds of chess and business have more similarities than you might think. Develop a plan, analyze the position, identify the weak points, and play with the end always in mind—these are concepts common to both worlds.

In my life in Spain (1928–1947), my life had only one dimension—chess. Instead of simply playing chess, I was "playing" high school and the first year of med school while studying chess. Although I was again playing chess in the early '70s, family and professional success were now the two focuses of my life, and chess was relegated to a hobby.

My business responsibilities continued to increase. I became responsible for the five molasses plants in the US and Canada (Montreal, Dartmouth, New Orleans, Wilmington, and Boston). I continued being a corporate vice president for Sucrest and the president of their Canadian subsidiary, Grandma Molasses ("*La Mélasse Grand-mère*"). During that time, I worked closely with my good friend Vince Amato, another vice president of Sucrest and a marketing genius—he converted Edible Molasses from a commodity sweetener sold by the gallon to a "specialty ingredient" sold by the pound!!

Vince was in charge of all sales of the specialty products in the US and had negotiated an agreement for the sale of the entire Grandma Molasses retail operations to Duffy-Mott (now known simply as Mott's), whose president was in love with our label and product line. Over my dead body—the Grandma retail brand was our most profitable product line in Canada! I fought like hell and won. Although the transaction went through for the US, Duffy-Mott agreed to exclude the Canadian market from the contract…with interesting long-term results. (Forty-five years later, in 2022, I just negotiated with *La Abuela Carmen*, my client in Spain, the rights to distribute Crosby Molasses in Europe. I am sure that the present owners of Crosby Molasses, who own the Grandma brand in Canada, are happy that I avoided selling the "Grand'Mere Molasses" brand back in the '70s.)

The workload was huge, but I liked what I was doing. I traveled a great deal within the US and Canada, to Brazil and the Caribbean, with some trips to Europe. The trips to Europe were frequently arranged so that I could stop and visit my family over the weekend and drive by the beautiful and famous *La Cibeles* fountain and plaza in the center of my beloved Madrid. In a way, every trip was an adventure.

Our family's quality of life was improving in parallel with my business success. Every year in the winter (sugar crop season), I would have to go to Barbados and Louisiana and the Dominican Republic. Having Bea's mother living with us gave us the flexibility to sometimes combine my work travel with a long weekend vacation with my wife.

My trips to Louisiana gave me an annual chance to practice my high school French with my friend Casimir Graugnard at what became a traditional molasses business luncheon. I never missed stopping for "Breakfast at Brennan's" to enjoy their delicious invention "Bananas Foster" and always took the opportunity to visit dear friends living in New Orleans. While in Louisiana, I needed to visit our small plant on North Gayoso Street (our suppliers of Edible Molasses from Louisiana), and occasionally the St. Mary Sugar Mill (our supplier of raw sugar for Sucrest's Chicago refinery). The Chicago refinery was unique: It only produced liquid syrups (both sucrose and invert) and received its supplies via the largest raw sugar warehouse in the world: the Mississippi River. The river was regularly full of barges in transit from Louisiana to the Chicago refinery.

I also made business trips to the Dominican Republic at least once per year from 1961 (when I had arranged the new supply source of Edible Molasses for the Sucrest Corporation) until 1990 when I retired (at age sixty-two) after thirty years with the Sucrest Company. These trips were always a pleasure. I had developed meaningful friendships at *Central Romana*, and visiting friends in the nearby capital city, Santo Domingo, was always an added pleasure. In addition, staying at the *El Embajador* hotel or having dinner at *Casa Lina* was worth the trip!

One of the highlights of the 1970s and my yearly visits to *Central Romana* was my being an eyewitness to the growth of their tourist paradise. *Casa de Campo* (Spanish for "country house") was developed in 1975 by Gulf & Western on seven thousand acres of its *Central Romana* sugar mill land. Because of our important long-term contract with *Central Romana* and the personal friendships we had developed,

Alvaro Carta (head of Gulf & Western's Americas Division) invited Bea and I to attend the official inauguration. (That was after he had participated in...or engineered...the takeover of South Puerto Rico Sugar Company by the giant conglomerate.)

Casa de Campo's famous golf course *"Dientes de Perro"* (Teeth of the Dog) opened in 1971. I still remember an afternoon in 1970 when VP Eduardo Martinez Lima invited me to go with him and meet the world-famous golf course designer, Pete Dye. Dye had just landed in Romana's corporate jet bringing a load of Kentucky grass for the golf course—they spared no expense in making this course top-notch.

Montreal

My frequent business travels to Montreal in the 1970s resulted in our family organizing a summer vacation in the Laurentian Mountains, north of Montreal. (I fondly remember the Chantecler Resort area in the early '60s, and later on the Gray Point.) Some of our favorite spots in Montreal were the classic Queen Elizabeth hotel, the "underground city" (which is so convenient for the harsh winters of Montreal), and dinners at *Les Filles du Roy*. We also visited the historic city of Quebec once—what a marvelous place!

By one of those coincidences of business and life, the 1976 Olympic Games were being held in Montreal. A year beforehand, tickets for the Games were made available for purchase. I thought it was a hell of a thing to be able to invite people to the Olympics in Canada, so I bought $10,000 worth of tickets and made reservations in different hotels (wherever I could) as a public relations investment for Sucrest's clients, suppliers, and people we wanted to treat. Starting with our big clients, I invited a lot of suppliers and customers alike.

Unfortunately (or fortunately!!), a few weeks before the games, one of the groups from Mexico who had accepted the invitation was unable to attend and canceled. After explaining the situation to my boss, we found a solution—my family (who had already had a vacation planned) could use the tickets to the Olympic Games! (I paid for the hotel myself, of course.) I feel very lucky to have been able to take my family, including Nonna, to the 1976 Olympics! Although our youngest, Robbie, was only three years old, I imagine the rest of the family has fond memories of the event.

Discovering the Westfield Chess Club

At the beginning of the 1970s, the Westfield Chess Club in central New Jersey was the strongest club in the region. Under the outstanding leadership of Denis Barry, its membership grew exponentially—Denis managed to attract the majority of the outstanding players in New Jersey.

I was honored when, in 1972, Denis invited me to participate in the first of a new series of "Invitational Tournaments" limited to the strongest players in New Jersey. I finished in third place, ahead of some of the strongest players, including Steve Stoyko, whom I beat in an interesting game. The tournament served to reconnect me with Steve Pozarek, the player I had faced in my first game after returning to chess in the New Jersey Open in 1968. That was the true beginning of our friendship, which still endures today.

In Westfield, Denis Barry formed a team that came to dominate the North Jersey Chess League during the 1970s and the early 1980s. I was an active participant in the league during the period. The monthly meetings allowed us to compete with strong opponents and offered us the opportunity to enjoy the interaction with the other members of the team. Steve Pozarek was the captain, and one of the strongest players was my friend, Wayne Conover. Wayne lived near me, and we generally went to the club meetings and matches together. Even after so many years, our friendship is as strong now as it was then.

Playing in Westfield also gave me the opportunity to meet a number of young talents who became very strong players after starting in the club. Among the outstanding players were John Fedorowicz (who became a Grandmaster), Mark Pinto (still active as a FIDE Master), and National Master Eugene Shapiro, a great player and an even better friend.

I frequently brought my sons to the club on Fridays after dinner. This became almost a sacred ritual for me. At 6 p.m., I would sit at our table for dinner, and ninety minutes later, I would go to the club. There, I would play a few games, discuss chess, and turn back into a teacher, sharing my knowledge of endgames with the younger players and often speaking about my experiences with Alekhine. In the following years, Steve Pozarek, Wayne Conover, and I formed the backbone of the team that prevailed every year in the NJ team league. The three of us have been club champions and formed such a close friendship that even after fifty years, we still get together once a month.

Despite my busy schedule, I was still able to participate in some large tournaments. I will always remember many things about that time—the games, the trips, the good moments, and especially the friendships. I am not including any of my chess games in this book since they are already published in either my articles in the Appendix, in my previous book *40 Years of Friendship: 100 Games of Chess* (written with Steve Pozarek and Wayne Conover), or in the book I published in Spain under the title *Jugando en el tablero de la vida* (*Playing on the Board of Life*, written with my co-author, Javier Cordero Fernandez).

In chess, I played hundreds of games. At the same time, I was playing many other games on the black-and-white squares of refined sugar and blackstrap molasses. In business, I was always looking to increase the profitability by developing value-added specialty products. I converted part of our blackstrap molasses (for animal feed) into the (then) new concept of "Liquid Feed," based on blackstrap molasses plus liquid urea as a source of protein (for ruminants only), minerals, and vitamins. My career was continuing to expand into new frontiers, and I was loving life.

Giving back to chess some of what it gave to me

In 1977, the frequency of my chess playing was decreasing, while I became more active as a coach and a lecturer; first, with my own children; later, with frequent lectures in the Westfield Club (and other clubs that invited me); and finally, as a volunteer trainer for high school clubs.

My love of chess started with my father's teachings and later traveled a long road full of curves, bumps, and many positive experiences. Of course, knowing all the good that chess can add to life, I taught my children to play. In addition, over the last fifty years, I have had the pleasure of teaching many other children to play and even coached high school teams.

I will never forget my first coaching experience at my own children's school. In 1978, Gene began attending the Christian Brothers Academy High School, and I became their volunteer coach. I am very proud of helping them to win, for the first time in their history, the New Jersey High School Championship title! My wife, Bea, worked in several schools with students with special needs. She would always recommend me as a volunteer trainer for chess clubs in the schools where she worked, and I never hesitated to accept. It was a very enriching experience—chess can help many people and can improve lives.

As a fifteen-year-old, World Champion Alekhine's comment about the role of chess in life remained with me forever. Over the decades since it occurred, I have repeated his advice many times, not only to the students that I helped to train as a high school coach but also to the chess clubs where I was a guest speaker. In my lectures about chess, I frequently also used my game against Alekhine as a lesson about the queen-knight teamwork in chess.

While busy with work, family, and coaching/lecturing, I still found time to play the Manhattan Chess Congress, where I was able to play an interesting game against the young master Joel Benjamin, who has since become one of the most respected GMs in the United States. I had faced Joel some years earlier (when he was a child prodigy at age eleven) during a match between the Westfield Club and the famous Manhattan Chess Club. Both games were draws. As a non-professional "club player," I remember both results proudly.

By 1976, the two older boys (Gene, fourteen, and Henry, ten) were pretty good chess players, and little brother Robbie at age three wanted to learn and play with his brothers. He learned at an incredible speed!

This decade was, for me, an absolute confirmation of what World Champion Alekhine said to me when I was fifteen—that there were things in life more important than chess. I was impressed (for life) and always told my children and students: Whether you become a chess master or not, make sure to be the master of your own life!!

CHAPTER 9:
The End of My Career as a Corporate Executive
(1980–1993)

Although the decade had changed, my life was largely the same. I continued to be very focused on my work for the Sucrest Corporation. In those days, I frequently traveled to Montreal and New Orleans, two cities that both have edible molasses and French history. (Montreal and the province of Quebec have the highest per capita consumption of cane juice molasses in the world, while Louisiana is the largest producer and consumer of edible molasses in the US.) During the 1980s, I was in charge of all the company's molasses plants, and in the world of fancy molasses and CJM (cane juice molasses), I had become a true master.

In chess, however, I was unable to develop much of a career, but enjoyed the challenge and my experiences.

My chess in the '80s

Due to my focus on my work, my participation in tournaments was limited to local events, almost always at the Westfield Club or in the quadrangular tournaments that my friend, the late Glen Petersen, organized on the weekends in New Jersey.

In one unusual experience in January 1980, I achieved a great result in the Westfield Chess Club's Rapid Tournament. It was near the beginning of the computer chess age, and one of the other participants was Bell Laboratories' world champion computer, Belle (designed by Ken Thompson of Bell Laboratories fame). The tournament was an entertaining fight in which I earned fourteen points in seventeen games, finishing in second place behind IM Mike Valvo but ahead of Belle (who would soon become the world champion of computers). The future was coming, and there was no stopping it, but, for one day of my lifetime, I had a better result than the future world champion computer!

King Salomon and his three knights

In 1980, I had one of my most cherished memories with chess—one of the moments I will always remember. Many of them are linked to family and are mostly the experiences you share with your children, as happened in 1980 when I decided to enter the US Amateur Team Chess Championship with my three sons. We created a team with an odd name, "King Salomon and his Three Knights," with me as the captain, well-supported by my three sons.

Robbie in 1981

The championship brought together around four hundred players on ninety-seven teams that competed for three days. Curiously, the winning team was composed of two Spanish players, José Saenz and José Cuchí (the well-known organizer of the New York Open), with the famous Grandmaster Roman Dzindzichashvili as captain.

My son Robbie, who hadn't yet turned seven, was the youngest player and was interviewed during the tournament. The journalist asked him a few questions that Robbie answered with a simple "*Yep*," until the journalist finally asked him this, "Do you know what 'concentration' means?" To which Robbie replied, "*Yep*. You sit on your hands and shut up."

In terms of chess, Robbie was a precocious child. While I was training his brothers, Gene (fourteen years old) and Henry (eight years old), to be on the chess teams at their schools, Robbie, who was only three years old, didn't miss a bit of what happened on those entertaining chessboards full of pieces that continually moved around. In the end, it was his brothers that taught him how to play. Robbie showed great ability to learn and progressed rapidly, so much so that he was the elementary school champion in New Jersey at age seven, after facing many opponents older than himself.

I recall a funny anecdote about Robbie. One time, at the end of the '70s, a friend visited us. He knew that I was a good player, and he mentioned that he would like to play a game against me. Since he was a good friend, I said, "Sure, Joe, but before playing me, you have to beat Robbie." Joe and I never got to play…and we still laugh about it when we see each other.

Similar to my own life, Robbie's life did not run along the track of chess. Today, he is a professor at the Stern School of Business at NYU, and he believes that chess helped him greatly as he was developing his capacity to reason, which applies to many situations in life. Indeed, chess has always been one of his hobbies; for example, while he was working on his doctorate in NYU (New York University), he would often show up to play at Washington Square Park, where there are chess boards available for anyone to use. And yes, by coincidence, it was the very same Washington Square Park that his mother and I had enjoyed while courting.

Following family tradition, Robbie taught chess to his two children, Ben and Sophie. Ben became part of a chess group at his school (Columbia Prep). The group was run by GM Michael Rohde, GM Joel Benjamin, and Sophia Rohde. So, you can see, chess has been present in my family for four consecutive generations—quite a distance from those long-ago years when chess helped my father during his time in prison and accompanied me when I moved twice to different countries. It has been a faithful companion.

Chess through three generations: Eugene, Robbie, and Ben (New York State Scholastic Championship)

Sporadic chess

Yes, chess was a faithful companion, but not the cornerstone of my life. Perhaps I didn't sit at a chessboard as often as I would have liked, but chess did fit perfectly into my life and gave me some great satisfaction. For example, in 1982, I succeeded in getting my name inscribed on the trophy of the Westfield Club by winning their annual tournament.

During the decade of the 1980s, Wayne Conover and Steve Pozarek would come to my home once a month. We played, analyzed positions, and spent a great deal of time in front of a chessboard. During one of those evenings, after learning that the US Open was going to be held in Somerset, New Jersey, that year, Wayne mentioned that we might be able to get back to playing serious tournaments. We were no longer young men, but the idea didn't fall on deaf ears. Since three of my children had already left for college, I had more free time, so the idea became a true challenge. I was close to fifty-eight years old but still had the same love for chess that I had in my youth. So, we decided to train.

Wayne and I began several months of intensive training. He is an international master in correspondence chess and had been part of the US team at the Olympiad in that capacity. He reached an Elo of over 2,400 points, so his opinion was very important when we were considering which chess openings to prepare. For our repertoire with White, we worked on the Averbakh Variation against the King's Indian, meanwhile, with Black, we chose the Caro-Kann Defense and the Dutch Defense with the Leningrad Variation. This was a solid opening that also gave good attacking possibilities depending on how the fight developed, and it was a defense we both knew. Not since my Madrid days had I prepared to play chess with such intensity.

From left: Wayne Conover, Steve Pozarek, and Eugene Salomon, analyzing the critical position of my game against Alekhine.

At the beginning of August, we went to Somerset, along with 528 other players—a field that contained 11 GMs, 16 IMs, 9 FMs, and 66 NMs. They had organized a veritable festival of chess, with conferences given by some players as well-known as Benkö, Spassky, Gurevich, and Kudrin. There were also many workshops related to chess, with banquets and parties almost every day. We had chosen a great place to start our new voyage—a tournament with an atmosphere where everything was adorned with black and white squares. The work we did to reach this new stage proved very fruitful; for the first time in my life, I did not get into time trouble in my games, nor did I waste important time thinking during the opening. This impacted very positively on my game, helping me to achieve important results such as the draw against IM Karl Burger and the victory against Adam Leif, US Champion (under eighteen) who I defeated using the Leningrad Variation of the Dutch Defense.

In 1987, I attended the World Open in Philadelphia. If the event in Somerset was a big party, the one organized in Philly was something colossal: 1,253 chess players decided to participate in this tournament, many attracted by the phenomenal prize money of $181,000. I was already familiar with this tournament; at the end of the '70s, I used to travel into Philadelphia with my sons to play in the World Open. For them, it was a real treat—not for the chess itself, but because they could go to McDonald's or Burger King, their favorite places for lunch and dinner…for three days in a row!

Curiously, over the next few years, I had very little participation in tournaments—the big Opens took at least two weeks. Even so, I was able to play two interesting games, against opponents Hanon Russell at the US First Action Championship in 1988, and Richard Lunenfeld in the US Amateur Chess Team Tournament in 1989. This would be the prelude to my best period in competitive chess—the '90s.

Work gets even busier

The excitement I wasn't getting through chess (at least not strongly enough) was provided by my work life. 1983 and 1984 were exceptional years in my life as an executive for Ingredient Technology Corporation (ITC), the successor to Sucrest. After the president of the largest division of the company (Specialty Products) announced his impending retirement, I was put in charge of those operations in addition to continuing as head of my division, Xtravim, which specialized in animal feed.

Suddenly, my group (Specialty Products and Xtravim) became the most important in the company, and I began to develop new

Chapter 9: The End of My Career as a Corporate Executive

businesses that frequently took me to Europe. It was common for me to visit Paris, Marseille, London, Frankfurt, Milan, or Zurich with the idea of opening new markets for our ingredients in the pharmaceutical or nutraceutical industry, or to secure supplies of malt extract from England, Finland, or Italy.

One Monday, in 1987, while I was traveling for ITC, I flew to Switzerland. I had a new Swiss customer for whom we had developed Edible Molasses flakes for the nutraceutical market, and we were going to explore other new ingredients and/or a joint business. I had asked Rudy Everstadt (my boss, president of ITC) to accompany me as the prospects truly were intriguing. We were supposed to have a dinner meeting with our client in Zurich—I was flying from Madrid (a weekend family visit), and Rudy was flying from London.

Upon arrival in Zurich, Rudy knew that the New York Stock Market had collapsed—the Black Monday of 1987—but I didn't know it yet. Our stock had dropped from $21 a share to $13, and we presumed we were going to be the target of an unfriendly takeover attempt. We canceled all the meetings and headed back to NY to figure out how to protect ourselves—that flight was a seven-hour trip of intense discussion. I suggested to Rudy (and he agreed) that an ideal "white knight" to come to our rescue was Alfy Fanjul. His group, Flo-Sun, had the available capital for an acquisition, we were already doing business with one of his companies (*Central Romana*), and therefore, ITC might be attractive to them. Back in Manhattan, I called Eduardo Martinez Lima, one of Alfy's VPs, and asked him if he could arrange a meeting with Alfy to explore the idea. He said sure, and the meeting was scheduled for a couple of weeks later in November.

Three days before the meeting, Rudy Everstadt called me—what we had been dreading had happened. We had received an official tender offer from Malt Products (a corporate rival) to buy the company. The lawyers advised us that once there was an offer on the table, Rudy, as the company president, could not participate in the meeting. He asked me to go alone and tone down the meeting with Alfy. I flew to Palm Beach and changed the presentation to say that we were "looking for new opportunities/and/or partnerships." Unfortunately, nothing came out of the meeting, and we hired an investment firm to explore

131

alternative offers. The eventual winner was Crompton & Knowles, with an offer of $29 per share.

1988—The business road continues and supposedly reaches its end

Time was passing—years of hard, fruitful, and satisfying work—but at the same pace, retirement was approaching. It is popularly believed that when you get to your sixties, you can't wait to retire, but that wasn't how I felt. I enjoyed my work, and retirement wasn't foremost in my mind. However, 1988 was a year of uncertainty: After thirty successful years at the Sucrest Corporation, which had changed its corporate name to Ingredient Technology (ITC), the company was acquired by Crompton & Knowles— a much larger company. I didn't know what to expect. Fortunately, I was protected by a "golden parachute" contract. (Typically, those contracts are to protect the key executives and provide assurances that even if the company is taken over, they will be protected by a separation contract.)

When we were taken over by Crompton & Knowles, the new company convinced me not to retire yet, to wait two years, and asked me to continue in charge of the division that I currently led in order to aid in the transition. They assured me that my compensation check would still be waiting for me at the end of those two years, and I would have the option to retire or continue in my position. The proposal was interesting, so I negotiated a new contract…at age sixty.

I guess that in order to make me feel wanted and welcome, they expanded my job responsibilities, entrusting the consolidation of exportation of flavors and other ingredients (primarily to Europe) to my group. I was responsible for the operations in Mexico and Canada and had also organized in the past several export initiatives of special ingredients to Europe.

On the surface, everything seemed very promising, but a conflict lurked in the background. Logically, being a much larger company, Crompton & Knowles had a different kind of corporate management style that wasn't exactly to my liking. The transition from being a big fish in a little pond to being a little fish in a big pond was a traumatic change. I felt limited, and it was not pleasant, so the idea of a change began to roll around in my brain.

Decision time

By early 1989, before the annual Barbados trip in February, the idea of leaving Crompton & Knowles had become firmly planted in my mind. I decided to bring Mike DeLuca, my financial VP, on the trip to Barbados for purposes of management transition. (Mike and I had met back in the mid-1970s when, fresh out of college, he joined us at Sucrest working for my dear friend Vince Amato). I was teaching Mike the ins and outs of the business so that he could take over when I left, and this was a perfect opportunity for him to meet Jim Crosby. Meeting with competitors on US soil was not a good idea since it is often associated with the possibility of price-fixing, so I had chosen to hold the meeting in Barbados. During the breakfast that I had arranged with Jim Crosby, I planted an idea: the possibility of selling the Grandma Molasses retail product line to Crosby with a long-term supply contract for the cane juice molasses. (A few years back, we had used a similar strategy when we sold the retail and the brand of Grandma Molasses in the US to the Duffy-Mott company, in conjunction with a long-term supply contract.)

It took several years for that idea to come to fruition, but today, Grandma Molasses in Canada is a market leader for the Crosby group. And with a satisfied smile, I see them today promoting the Fancy Molasses from the *Madre Tierra* sugar mill in Guatemala—the plant I had originally designed and started up as a consultant! What a small world!

That meeting took place in Bridgetown in 1989, coincidentally, the same year that Fancy Molasses in Barbados decided to stop producing their molasses. I guess sugar and molasses could no longer compete with the value of real estate on the island. The annual Crosby and ITC February trip to Barbados that year turned into a farewell dinner with both our friends from Barbados Fancy Molasses and our Canadian friends from Crosby Molasses. The gracious organizers were Ron Innis and his wife, Ivonne. As I write this, I can look up and see on my desk the silver letter opener that Jim Crosby gave all the assistants at that dinner, which bears this inscription, "Haselton, Canada 23 S". It is a beautiful reminder of that era.

A big celebration

My sixty-second birthday, September 29, 1990, was certainly one to remember and the highlight of the year.

Through chess, I spent a lot of time with our sons, but I have, over the years, tried to find ways to spend significant time with my daughter, Maria. Two special times that I will always remember are our father-daughter brunch at Tavern on the Green in Central Park when she was a teenager, and the day some years later that we celebrated together—my sixty-second birthday fell on Maria's wedding day!

The emotion of walking her down the aisle in church on the day of her wedding was overwhelming. I jokingly thanked her for throwing such a big celebration for my birthday, but I was thrilled and honored to share such a special day with her.

My career takes a turn

Eduardo Martinez Lima, VP of *Central Romana*, knew that I was considering either retiring or starting a new career, and he recommended to Alfy that he should meet with me. One day, Eduardo called me and told me that Alfy Fanjul, Chairman of Flo-Sun, wanted to meet me at the Plaza Hotel. After discussing industry and specialty products, Alfy asked me to send him a resume. I replied, "To tell you the truth, Alfy, I have never had to prepare a resume." Fine, he said, and asked me to write a few lines about my experience and send it to him.

Chapter 9: The End of My Career as a Corporate Executive

A few weeks later, Eduardo called me and said, "Alfy tells me that there is an opening coming up as general manager of Okeelanta," which was the best sugar mill in North America. (During the crop season, Okeelanta Mill grinds twenty thousand tons of sugarcane per day— about one thousand trucks full of cane sugar every day!) I wasn't interested—I had already done mill management in Cuba and still had my contract at Crompton & Knowles until 1990. I called Martinez Lima, thanked him for the offer, and explained to him why I was not interested.

A few months later, Eduardo called again and said, "I was talking with Alfy. We want to create a new position to develop new specialty products from sugar. Would you be interested in being in charge of that?" Oh, yes—that intrigued me! That's how I was hired by Alfy Fanjul for this new position, to start January 1990, as VP of Okeelanta Sugar Co., VP of Osceola Farms (both in Florida), and VP of *Central Romana*—a position that I had turned down almost thirty years earlier! (If that is not a crazy coincidence, I do not know what is.) Exactly after the two years for which I was contractually bound to Crompton & Knowles, I left with a firm offer for a truly challenging position in hand…at age sixty-two!

That is how my new position, headquartered in Palm Beach, Florida, began. My main focus was developing value-added specialty sugar products for these three sugar mills, all owned or controlled by Flo-Sun. I worked alongside the GMs of the three sugar mills, reporting directly to Alfy for the Florida properties (Osceola and Okeelanta) and to Eduardo Martinez Lima for operations in the Dominican Republic. When he hired me, Alfy's instructions were to focus first on Osceola (Okeelanta already had programs in place) and that he was very "risk-averse," so I should keep that in mind when proposing new projects.

The first week of January 1990, I arrived at my beautiful office at Royal Poinciana Plaza in Palm Beach and had to figure out what to do and how to start. This was my first position in new business development, and I was not an expert in the field. My boss, Alfy Fanjul, was much too busy, so I was on my own.

I decided that my first priority was to visit every operation and meet all key management executives to try to identify opportunities, seek cooperation, and offer my help. During the first few weeks, I went to Okeelanta, and to my surprise, I found they had a small sugar refinery (something like a couple of hundred tons per day, which is like a pilot plant) and that all the production was under a private label contract with Savannah Sugar. Then I visited Osceola where I found the general manager, Mr. Jackson, quite receptive to any new program we could develop. Next, I went to Sem-Chi, a small rice factory—another incredibly small industrial unit. (My recollection is that the total capacity of the rice mill was fifty thousand hundredweight per year—much, much less than the output of any average rice mill in the country.)

I also started calling my network contacts to let them know about my new challenge in the industry and that I would love to explore any ideas we could develop together. All of a sudden, a beautiful coincidence came to my rescue. I contacted an old friend, Ira Katz, Corporate VP of IFF (International Flavors and Fragrances) who was in charge of research and development. Ira and I had a great relationship from the days when I was the chairman of the board of advisors at Rutgers University Department of Food Science, and he was the secretary. We had talked once about the extremely valuable natural aromatic micro-ingredient Damascenone (an exotic type of ingredient with a value over $1000/lb.), and his thinking was that sugarcane could possibly be a source. Remembering that conversation, I approached him, and we agreed to meet at the annual meeting of the IFT (Institute of Food Technologists).

A couple of weeks later, Jackson, the then-manager of Osceola, called me and said he had two visitors from IFF, referred to him by the "Florida Molasses Exchange." They came and were interested in investigating natural flavors from sugar. I told him, "By all means. Offer them an open house, show them everything. I want to meet them." One was Allen Pittet, in charge of natural flavors at IFF, a true scientist and PhD from England. His teammate, Marv Schulman, had worked in product and process research with General Foods for years. It was a

Chapter 9: The End of My Career as a Corporate Executive

privilege to work closely with them for several years both in Osceola and, later on, in *Central Romana*.

Keeping in mind that my boss, Alfy Fanjul, had told me about his risk-averse management style, I had a serious conversation with Ira Katz. I offered him our full support for a research program if they wanted to install a pilot plant to research possible natural ingredients from the cane sugar industry. I told him we would provide the infrastructure, the cost of operation, and all the manufacturing support they might need, but I could not commit to any financial investment in the pilot plant. "All I need, Ira, is your technical direction and the pilot plant investment. I do not have an R&D budget and, as my first project, I need to present a long-term project without the risk of capital investment to our chairman. You will have our 100-percent cooperation." Ira told me that they had been exploring the idea in Louisiana but that he would be very happy to discuss a formula of mutual interest with us. Ira then put me in touch with Mr. Keimig, who was the head of purchasing to negotiate the agreement. Obviously, lawyers were also involved, but that meeting between Keimig, Ira, and myself resulted in a seven-year contract with IFF for a pilot plant at Osceola Farms.

Once we entered the seven-year contract, sometime in 1991, a pilot plant was built at Osceola, 100-percent financed and designed by IFF, for the isolation and production of the first identified product—natural DMS (dimethyl sulfide) This product, at the time, commanded a price between $150 to $400/kg. Unbelievably, in the first days of his visit to our Osceola Farms plant, Allen, with his incredible olfactory ability, identified the odor of DMS. We were still in our first year of the contract when we started producing the natural DMS. As a follow-up, we began to work on a couple of other projects: "Molasses Distillate" and a valuable flavor modifier obtained by distillation of the cane sugar leaves ("Cane Leaves Distillate").

After our success at Osceola, I took the IFF team to *Central Romana*. First, we investigated recovering natural acetic acid from their Furfural production plant. It was an ambitious project as we not only would obtain a valuable organic ingredient, but we would also simultaneously solve what was then a serious pollution problem. It would work if we changed the process from using sulfuric acid to using phosphoric acid…but Dr. Louis Smith, head of the Furfural operations, vetoed the concept, and that was the end of what I thought was a promising idea.

A second area of research was related to an international company based in Spain called Campofrio, which specializes in pork products. They had a multi-million-dollar joint venture in *Central Romana*, where a Campofrio plant processed Dominican pork into cold cuts. After a long investigation, the results were remarkable. IFF suggested they could put up a plant next to Campofrio to extract natural flavors from all the cold cuts' processing. Sometime in the early 1990s, IFF was so impressed with the potential of this project that we organized a trip to *Central Romana*—the president of IFF and three of his key managers flew to meet with us at *Central Romana* to discuss what would have been a major breakthrough.

Unfortunately, life coincidences are not always good. Just as we were working on the project, there was a scare about potential pork cholera in the Dominican Republic, so the importation of cold cuts from Campofrio's Dominican Republic plant into the US was stopped. That resulted in the end of Campofrio's operations in Romana, and the death of my happy dreams of a major success there. After that, I worked on some minor programs related to tropical fruits in Romana, but nothing of note.

Those were three exciting years during which I contributed to the conversion of a basic commodity-oriented company into one that would refine its own sugars and become a world leader in edible molasses and other value-added specialties. I also helped to develop their rice operations. I was truly happy, but my wife was not, being so far away from our children and grandchildren.

In 1993, due to family considerations, I told Alfy that I had to retire and return to New Jersey, even though the contract with IFF had four more years to go. He was quite impressed by how fast we had developed DMS, and he knew we were working on additional "natural ingredients." Alfy wanted me to remain in charge, so he offered me a consulting contract. It was a blessing—all of a sudden, I became a consultant…for the next thirty years!

CHAPTER 10:
The Consultant Years
(1993 and Beyond)
A new business career

In 1993, after forty years as an executive in the sugar and food industry, I retired at age sixty-five from the corporate world. My three-year contract as VP creating "value-added products" for three large sugar mills (two in Florida and one in the Dominican Republic) from the corporate office in Palm Beach had ended, but an exciting new career as a consultant began with a four-year contract as a "dedicated" consultant was just beginning.

The transition's origin—successfully organizing a seven-year R&D program with giant flavor company, IFF—resulted in some new, intriguing products. My first call as a consultant was to my old, good friend Mike DeLuca (then vice president at Crompton & Knowles) to offer my consulting services. I knew they were going to need new sources of CJM supply because the contract that I had initiated thirty years earlier with *Central Romana* was being discontinued. (Romana had a new project that was much more profitable.) Sure enough, Mike contracted me as a consultant to help him develop new sources of supply. It was a repetition of my previous project with Sucrest thirty-four years earlier, when in 1960, I had investigated the Caribbean and Mexico to replace Cuba as the CJM (cane juice molasses) source of supply and had selected *Central Romana*, Dominican Republic. This time, however, in 1994, I traveled to Brazil, Colombia, and Central America, finally settling on Guatemala, where I designed a plant, trained the personnel, and helped Mike to negotiate a long-term contract.

With Crompton & Knowles as my second client, I then called my friend Felipe Suberbie in Mexico (head of *"Complementos Alimenticios"*—Food Ingredients), with whom I had an excellent business relationship over many years. They became my third client, and that was enough. I did not need any more clients!

My consulting and friendly relationships with C&K and Florida Crystals resulted, years later, in my helping Luis Fernandez, my teammate at Florida Crystals, to recruit Mike DeLuca to develop the area of natural and organic ingredients business. (He later became a VP, running the Specialty Products under Domino's umbrella.) What an outstanding job Mike did! I felt incredibly proud when he invited me to his retirement dinner party that Domino Foods organized in New Jersey on September 28th, 2017…the day before my eighty-ninth birthday. Beatrice and I were the only outsiders joining the Domino New Jersey staff for the event. After working together closely in different capacities over the past thirty-three years, I felt quite honored when he referred to me as his friend and his mentor.

As a consultant, my personal life improved. The business did well and permitted me the luxury of being selective about what projects I worked on. This resulted in several interesting experiences, including, in 2014, being contracted by Navajo Pride (the agro-industrial group of the Navajo Nation) to help them develop a five-year business plan. And the projects kept coming: Some were really attractive, such as the opportunity for production of organic rice syrup. In cooperation with my Mexican client, Felipe Suberbie, and his company, *Complementos Alimenticios*, we brought truckloads of organic rice from Florida to their plant in Querétaro, México, to a grain extraction plant that we had upgraded to conform to organic standards. There, we produced rice syrup, which was then sent to California for the production of nutritional bars. The project went very well, but it was not long before the Chinese and Pakistani companies began doing it at much lower prices, crushing all my plans.

My career in the sugar industry was a most pleasant adventure: eight years of technical/management experience in Cuba's sugar industry, followed by an exciting thirty-year-long management career in New York with the Sucrest Corporation and its successors, and three final years in Florida, helping the leading raw sugar company change focus from being purely a commodity sugar to becoming an independent sugar refiner, while developing the area of "value-added specialty products". Then, by coincidences of life, and thanks to hard work and good relationships built over the years, those wonderful experiences were followed by three additional decades of consultant work.

CHAPTER 11:
The End of my Competitive Chess Life
(1993–99)

I wanted to have some time free to make a last try with my then-fifty-year passion—chess. Luckily, my new work as a consultant gave me the flexibility to schedule my own work and allowed me to try for a late revival of my teenage years' chess career. Curiously enough, after age sixty-five, I played some of the best games of my life!

One of my first destinations was a well-known tournament in Spain: "The International Open of the Principality of Asturias," held in Oviedo, Spain, in December of 1993. My participation in the Oviedo tournament had been Pablo Morán's idea, who recommended that I play not only because of the wonderful atmosphere that had occurred at the previous year's event but also because of the high number of great players who were participating. Pablo took care of everything and invited me to stay at his apartment during those days, which I happily accepted. I got on a plane to my beloved Asturias to compete along with such renowned players as Judit Polgar, Timman, Anand, Salov, Bronstein, Portisch, Ivkov, Najdorf, and Averbakh. I didn't play very well, but the important thing was the days spent with Morán. It was the last meeting of two "lifelong and forever" friends as Pablito himself described our friendship.

The Open tournaments

Back in the US, I started playing all the major Open tournaments (the New York Open, the World Open in Philadelphia, the National Open in Las Vegas, the Chicago Open) and as many others as I could attend. Consulting enabled me to continue enjoying my business activity while finally being able to dedicate serious time to my then-half-century-long passion.

These Open tournaments often had hundreds of participants in a mix of amateurs and masters—a truly interesting concept that allows us amateurs to play against the professionals. Starting in 1994, my performance improved, and I had a nice increase in my rating, which rose to 2, 289 points (not too bad for a sixty-five-year-old senior!). The quality of my games at sixty-five was even better than it was in my youth, when I could beat Spanish champions such as Antonio Medina or F.J. Perez (during 1945–47), or Cuban champions such as Rogelio Ortega and Gilberto Garcia (in 1952).

In 1995, I went to the capital of the gaming world, Las Vegas, to participate in the National Open. I remember this tournament above others for the great results I achieved against the masters that I faced. Not only did I draw with GM Arthur Bisguier, IM Anthony Saidy, WIM Anjelina Belavskokaya, and Brazilian master David Borensztajn, I defeated Latvian FM Viktor Pupols!

Out of all my tournament appearances in 1997, I especially remember the World Open in Philadelphia. It was a very challenging tournament, with a high number of titled players. Despite all that, I finished above the midpoint of the standings, and with an even score.

The farewell…or not: Anibal Open of Linares, 1998

In this life, everything has a beginning and an end, including life itself, and in 1998, at age seventy, I knew that the time had come to put an end to my competitive chess career. Considering that, I wanted to find a special tournament to close out this beautiful journey that had allowed me to have such enjoyable experiences. I also knew that I

Chapter 11: The End of my Competitive Chess Life

wanted it to be in Spain, where it all began, closing the circle around the square board.

I decided to consult with my old friend Mauricio Perea, who I had met many years earlier in the 1968 New Jersey Open. (Mauricio and I had developed a close relationship after discovering we had very similar backgrounds. Both our families had suffered the consequences of the 1936–1939 Spanish Civil War—his family emigrated to Mexico; mine went to Cuba)—and we both eventually relocated to the US. He went on to have a successful career in the pharmaceutical industry, while mine was in the food industry. Many years later, I became a strong master in New Jersey, and he did the same in Texas.)

After we met in New Jersey, we continued our friendship with dinners in Manhattan. A few years later, he called me, excited—he was returning to our native Spain with a high management position in the pharmaceutical industry…and we remained in touch for years.

Mauricio strongly recommended that I should play the Anibal Open in Linares, Spain. I learned from him that, while playing at a previous Linares Open, he and his wife, Ines, had dinner with the future World Champion Viswanathan Anand, which had developed into a very close friendship…something like a second father in Spain (in "Vishy's" words). I took Mauricio's advice and registered for the tournament.

Some of the students from the Instituto de Jovellanos (my high school) during a meal in Gijón. Manolín is second from right, and I am fourth from right.

Once the tournament started, a wonderful surprise awaited me. When Manuel "Manolín" González Rico, my first school friend from age ten in Gijón, heard that I would be playing in the Aníbal Open, he got in his car and drove several hours from Madrid to Linares so we could seize the rare opportunity to see each other once again.

I had shared many games of barefoot soccer with Manolín (nephew of the outstanding Asturias chess champion, Antonio Rico) on the beach at San Lorenzo during my childhood, and some games of chess at my house near Parque Begoña.

The tournament play was interesting on a personal level. I earned good results, especially the victory (after a beautiful tactical fight) against Gabriel Sargissian, World Youth Chess Champion (under twelve). It may have taken me fifty-four years, but after my 1944 loss to World Champion Alekhine, I could now claim a victory against another world champion (even if he was in the "under twelve" category.) I was honored that this game was selected by *Chess Informant #71* as a game with one of the best combinations of that quarter-year from around the world.

I also played (and should have drawn) my game against the sensation of the tournament, Chinese player, WGM Pin Wang (who began to compete in the third round and scored seven points in eight games). Unfortunately, a small error in the ending resulted in a loss. Regardless, perhaps the most rewarding aspect was the creative chess I was able to play at age seventy. Those games included interesting combinations and were supposed to be a nice end to my career on the chessboard.

During the ten days of the tournament, I had time to enjoy myself in Linares: I visited the bullfighting ring where a famous Spanish bullfighter, Manolete, died in 1947. I also became familiar with the immense olive fields there—a landscape so very different from what I had known and experienced in my younger years in Northern Spain.

It was an unforgettable experience that had a wonderful ending when my old friend from Madrid, Eladio Benito, offered to take me back to the capital. Manuel D'Agustín, a famous journalist and chess master, also joined us. During the trip, D'Agustín and I played a game of blindfolded chess, where you do not need a board since both players can remember the entire board and the pieces. Manuel was sitting in the backseat, and I was in the front seat. The game lasted almost the

Chapter 11: The End of my Competitive Chess Life

entire four-hour car ride, and I ultimately won, thanks to a well-played ending.

I had planned to end my chess career in Spain where it started—but it did not quite work out that way. I wound up playing a few more tournaments in the United States and ending my individual chess career at the National Open in Las Vegas, in March of 1999.

A photo with a great deal of significance: Here are the pieces that Alekhine used in Gijón in 1944, on the chessboard given to participants in the National Open in Las Vegas in 1999, showing the critical position from my game against IM Rogelio Ortega, played in Havana in 1952.

Upon my return home after the Aníbal Open in Linares, I received an envelope from the US Chess Federation. Inside the envelope was a certificate dated February 28, 1998—it was my title of Life Master! That title, which is quite difficult to earn, proudly hangs in my office at home…just in front of me as I am typing these lines.

CHAPTER 12:
24 Years of Life after 70

I was leaving chess behind, and at seventy years old, I was a complete beginner in a new world—computers. I wanted to learn so that I could explore what it looked like in "the future," and at the same time, create a database of my most significant games. I first had to learn how to use the Chessbase program and then choose my most interesting games (I selected some 140). Reviewing all my handwritten books, each with a few hundred games, to select the ones I liked best was a very, very time-consuming project! In addition to the chess game database, I created a collection of a few hundred pictures scanned from old family albums and saved my record albums in a digital format. (Not bad for an old guy!) This is how, years later, I was able to transfer them to my iPhone and listen to them in my car.

I also archived on my desktop videos of the beautiful places where I had lived: Gijón, Madrid, Havana, and New York (*Gijón del alma*; *El chotis de Madrid*; *New York, New York*), along with a beautiful video of Havana. I invested a great deal of time in these projects, and they have brought me so much joy.

I have always been very fond of photography and used to belong to our community photography club (Greenbriar Woodlands) of which I was president in 1995. Through this club, expert photographers were invited to give presentations and exhibits, and we took trips to picturesque spots to enjoy taking pictures. On one occasion, I organized a presentation of 150 of my slides, under the title "From Spain with Love". It was well-attended since many people were interested in the subject.

Two of my favorite photographs: **Left:** Picture taken in Oviedo, Spain, which won a prize in my photography club in New Jersey
Right: Seen on the street while visiting Los Picos: "The Cat Guarding the Henhouse"

I continued with these activities long after retirement, while also taking part in social media and learning to use my iPhone (thanks to my grandson Ben). At age seven or eight, he taught me how to navigate those new and frustrating waters, while I taught him how a knight jumps across a chessboard.

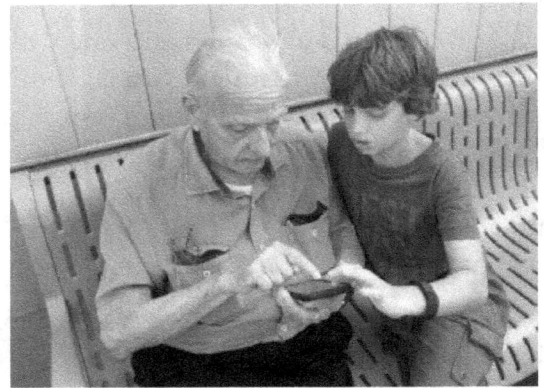

Ben and I

Chapter 12: 24 Years of Life after 70

Meeting World Chess Champion GM Garry Kasparov in 2014. **Left**: I am showing him the group picture taken in Gijon seventy years ago of me with another giant of chess, World Champion Alexander Alekhine. **Right**: Later that evening at a cocktail party

I have also been able to participate in multiple conferences and promotional events organized by various chess clubs, for which I readily volunteer without hesitation. I owe a debt of gratitude to chess, not only for how much I enjoyed it but also for how much it has helped me in life—teaching me reasoning, patience, and perseverance.

Gene playing a simultaneous exhibition against six children and six senior citizens at the Toms River Chess Club, circa 2017.

The Toms River Chess Club

The conference I remember most fondly was one I participated in several days before my ninetieth birthday with the Toms River Chess Club—which was supposed to be my last lecture. As a surprise, the club turned the conference into a birthday party for me! The president of the club, Steve Shoshin, had invited one of the club's original members—my old friend, Steve Doyle. His job was to introduce me and tell some stories of the things we have shared over the years. Steve (Doyle) and I met at the Westfield Chess Club in the 1970s and had accumulated shared experiences up until the end of the 1990s. That was when he published an account of my game against the Russian master Lenar Murzin (who played in the World Open in Philadelphia in 1998) in his newspaper chess column.

Steve informed the audience that although I was ninety, I was not the oldest presenter in the club since the famous Edward Lasker had given a talk when he was ninety-two years old. I promised him that I would happily return to the club in three years if they invited me! (As of this writing, I have an invitation to give my last chess conference this September—soon after this book is published so that we can combine it with a book signing.)

The Toms River Chess Club—I am kneeling farthest forward.

Chapter 12: 24 Years of Life after 70

Playing blindfold chess at age eighty-nine

In 2017, I agreed to participate in the events the Toms River Chess Club had organized for the city's 250th birthday celebration. One of the players was Jack Silver, a thirteen-year-old talent who had been a student of Leonid Yudasin, and who, at ten years old, had an Elo rating of 1681. He had achieved several wins in junior tournaments, had taken second place in the US Junior Grand Prix, and was my opponent in an exhibition game that day.

Truthfully, I don't recommend that anyone try it at that age—blindfold chess takes great mental effort and can be exhausting. I lost that game, but it did not matter much—it was a day to enjoy. The city cordoned off the main street of town, and among the many stands along the street was ours, where several chess players sat at boards ready to play anyone who approached. After seeing the picture (below) posted on social media, historian and writer Miguel Ángel Nepomuceno commented, "Quite an achievement for Gene, at an age greater than any world master, including Mieses. Congratulations!"

Me playing blindfold chess against young chess sensation, Jack Silver, at the celebration of the founding of the city of Toms River

During the event, I had the opportunity to chat at length with Jack's parents. Some days later, I invited them to our home, and we spent another very pleasant day together. After showing Jack and his brother one of my games, Jack, who always wants to move the pieces on the chessboard, asked me if we could play a fast game, so we did. Of course, as I do on special occasions, we played with Alekhine's pieces. This time, the victory fell on my side, even though, as with the other game, the outcome mattered little. The important thing was sharing my vision of chess with a young player just beginning his journey through this game. I couldn't help giving him a bit of advice that is always in the back of my mind: "Do not focus exclusively on becoming a chess master. Work on making yourself a master of life."

Three years later, when I contacted them to discuss that day (in preparation for this book you have in your hands), Jack replied that those words had really stayed with him. He said he had actively pursued other hobbies away from the chessboard and had found a new passion for writing, especially fiction stories and scripts. He also wrote something that touched me, "Being a master of life is more than just a wise piece of advice—it is a goal, an objective to which we should all aspire. If we do it well enough, it is something that never ends, and you keep pursuing it your entire life."

A Spaniard in a New Jersey Hall of Fame

Toms River Chess Club has its own Hall of Fame and has inducted several great names from the past who have given simultaneous sessions or presentations for the club. These include Botvinnik, Tal, Petrosian, and Karpov, as well as some more recent names—Caruana, Nakamura, and Kamsky. I feel privileged that my name was also included in the Club's Hall of Fame—a good group to be part of!

Steve Shoshin, president of the Toms River Chess Club (TRCC), wrote an article celebrating my ninetieth birthday and my seventy-five years of chess, and explained, "Gene has given a series of conferences and simultaneous exhibitions, and has helped the revitalized TRCC to grow and prosper. For this reason, and for his extraordinary career in chess, we award him a spot in our Hall of Fame."

Steve Doyle and Gene Salomon with the Toms River Chess Club's Hall of Fame plaque in 2018.

A veteran team

As I said at the beginning of this chapter, during these years, I always kept chess by my side—sometimes very closely, as occurred during the tournament of the United States Amateur Team East in 2020, held at the Hilton in Parsippany, NJ. It was the tournament's fiftieth anniversary, so we couldn't miss it…and we were not alone. 1,400 total players, comprising 325 teams, took over the hotel.

One of the reasons I participated was to be able to outline a project I was planning for the end of the year—a conference that would celebrate the fiftieth anniversary of chess in New Jersey under the auspices of the Toms River Chess Club. For this purpose, I had assembled a team of chess personalities (historians, teachers, and players). My plan was that Steve Doyle (tournament organizer for over forty years) would be my main speaker, then historian Peter Tamburro, Leroy Dubeck (treasurer of the *Chess Foundation),* Glen Petersen (tournament organizer), and Dr. Richard Lewis (a chess teacher for over thirty years) would also speak. It was projected that the conference would be videotaped for the archives of the US Chess Federation (as offered by my panelist Leroy Dubeck). Unfortunately, all the plans were canceled with the arrival of the coronavirus. Can we someday revisit the idea of having this conference about chess in New Jersey? I hope so! We have a rich history that is worth keeping alive. I only hope that the crisis eventually disappears and permits someone to develop this idea. I offer myself voluntarily if I am still here!

At ninety-one years of age, I was the captain of 'The Oldest Team in Town', composed of veteran players from Toms River and Westfield—at an average age of seventy-one: Gregory Coats, the youngest (at sixty-one); Edd Knowles, sixty-six; Richard Lewis, seventy-seven; Gene Salomon, ninety-one; and Mark Pinto, sixty-three.

Members of "The Oldest Team in Town"

As captain of the team, I arranged in advance that the alternate player would play three of my games, so I only had to play one game per day. (That way, I could promise my friends and family that I wouldn't lose more than three games!) I was pleasantly surprised—I did not lose any games (two ties and one win), and the team performed well overall.

The experience was most pleasant. I was able to return to competing after twenty-one years, and I did it alongside old friends from the Westfield Chess Club and more recent friends from the Toms River

Chapter 12: 24 Years of Life after 70

Chess Club. For being the oldest player among the 1,400 present, I was recognized and given a book as a prize.

This type of tournament offers more than simply playing some games and competing: It gives players the opportunity to reconnect with old friends they would not otherwise have the opportunity to see. That's what happened for me with Dr. Richard Lewis, who is an institution at the Westfield Club. Dr. Lewis, a dentist by trade, was a chess teacher for thirty-six years, and even volunteered in Africa to teach chess to children with HIV. On my first night in the hotel, I was walking with Richard, talking, when suddenly a man ran up to us who we instantly recognized—it was Dave Lazarus, longtime member of the Westfield Club.

From left to right—David Lazarus, Eugene Salomon, and Richard Lewis

Smiling, he said, "I wanted to take a picture with the two of you! Gene, I will never forget your conferences about endings. I learned so much, and they were an inspiration." I was amazed and even touched by his words: When you stand in front of a group of young people and try to teach them something as complex as chess, you never really know if the message reaches them, or even if you are successful in getting their attention. It is truly gratifying to sometimes have proof that the connection was successful, and the message got through.

Recently, Joshua M. Anderson, president of Chess Journalists of America, asked me to author some articles for their quarterly website magazine. My first article for the April 2022 publication highlighted a few of the games I played between sixty-five and seventy years of age. My eighty-year-long career as an amateur chess master is full of coincidences and anecdotes, but some of the most important, those nearest and dearest to my heart, are described in those articles mentioned in Appendix B.

Left: Gene and Joshua working on one of Gene's articles for CJA.
Right: Gene, Diane, and Joshua

My other senior hobby/pastime—Bridge

Bridge has become my new passion in the last fifteen years when I started to play sanctioned tournaments of duplicate bridge.

I learned to play bridge in Havana, in 1952, where I used to play every Sunday after Mass (still in Latin) on the beautiful patio of the ACU. These weekly meetings were always with friends, including Ángel Fernández Valera, the same one who introduced me to Fidel Castro on my first day in the country, back in late November 1947, the day of my arrival from Spain on the *M/T Magallanes*.

In 1956, we moved our weekly games to Ángel's house. The host himself asked me to partner with him, which I did from that moment on. Ángel was the director of the newspaper *El Mundo*, as well as a leader of the political right in Cuba. Our meetings continued until late 1959, when his house was placed under surveillance as he was suspected of being a counterrevolutionary. As a result, he decided to cancel our games so as not to compromise any of us who played there.

(It turns out that G-2, the Military Intelligence Service, or State Security, was not mistaken. Ángel was part of the Cuban counter-revolution, which I discovered when he, knowing that I was an engineer, asked me to interpret some aerial reconnaissance photos that had been secretly taken. I had already suffered through the calamities of a civil war and did not want to get involved in another, so I said, "Ángel, I lived through the Spanish Civil War—a second one is not for me." I then suggested another agricultural engineer who I knew was sympathetic to the cause. "Who?" he quickly asked. "Rogelito," I responded. We were talking about Rogelio Gonzalez Corzo, a friend from the ACU, who used to visit me frequently at *Central Providencia* under the pretense of selling chemical fertilizer. What I could not have suspected at that time was that only a few months later, Rogelio would become a martyr for the counter-revolutionary anti-Castro movement and would be shot by order of Castro. It was a story I lived first-hand, and a most painful one.)

In the United States, I had achieved the title of Life Master in chess and have now also achieved the title of Bridge Life Master. After receiving my Bridge Life Master title in 2012, I slowed down my traveling to the big tournaments, so it took me until recently (2021) to reach 1,000 points. That earned me the difficult-to-achieve title of Silver Life Master…at age ninety-four.

Rober, my nephew and my partner whenever I visit Madrid to play at Eurobuilding (a prestigious European bridge club site) or some weekend tournaments on the internet, describes our "partnership" as follows:

> *"My uncle Gene had never spoken to me about bridge during my time in America. When I started to practice with him, I learned that he began playing as a university student in Havana, and had returned to bridge after retiring from chess in 1999. We soon began to share this new passion, albeit on opposite sides of the Atlantic, thanks to*

the internet. When I started playing bridge with him, I saw from the first moment that his experience and expertise at imagining the possible combinations of cards could work in our favor and would allow us to get excellent results more frequently. Bridge was added to our extensive list of shared hobbies and passions. He helped me see the beauty and nuance of the game, leading me to appreciate it more than I had initially, and was instrumental in my "bridge-istic formation." We enjoyed many tournaments together, particularly playing in the International Championship of Gijón in 2009."

Curiously enough, even my passion for duplicate bridge (a competitive form of bridge which is a true source of pleasure and challenge in my old age) has some roots in my childhood with my mother. During the years after the Spanish Civil War, my grandfather and his two daughters (my mother and my aunt Lucrecia "Cachita," who by then was a widow living with my grandfather), enjoyed playing "Tresillo," a card game.

Unable to go downstairs to play in the park because of the war, I would spend hours watching them play cards…and learned how to play well!! Tresillo is a game with *subasta* (the bidding process where one bets as to how many tricks you can make in your choice of *triunfo*—trump). Thinking about it, I believe that my childhood familiarity with the "bidding strategies" was undoubtedly helpful in my becoming a Bridge Life Master after only a few years of playing duplicate bridge tournaments. Many years later, when we were reunited with my mother in Cuba (1948 to 1952), we used to play canasta, another card game that she loved.

To this day, I continue to play bridge, both in my bridge club and on the internet. It is not only a beautiful challenging game, but I am also sure that it helps we seniors to keep our minds sharp.

Golden Anniversary

On December 3, 2011, Bea and I were blessed to celebrate fifty years of marriage. Obviously, a fiftieth wedding anniversary is something notable and remarkable, and we decided that the best way to celebrate would be with our first priority—our family. Proud of our four children and seven grandchildren (ages six to sixteen), we elected to take a Disney cruise as a celebration that our grandchildren would never forget. It was a marvelous reunion—a cruise specifically designed for children and their families. In all, it was a wonderful experience to share with our children and grandchildren, and some of them still talk about the possibility of repeating it. It definitely helped to create a bond between the grandchildren who live in various parts of the country and was a very practical way of maintaining family tradition.

My father would be happy and proud looking at this picture.

Another visit to Spain

In 2017, Bea and I took Nina, one of our California granddaughters, to Spain on a working vacation—New York to Madrid, Córdoba, Seville, Madrid, and back to New York—what a trip! We introduced Nina to her roots in Madrid, Spain—she met many of the Salomon cousins and great-aunts. Next, we visited Córdoba. We had been invited a couple of years earlier by Manuel Vaquero Ortiz, a business consulting client and friend. What a treat!! We were privileged to visit "*La Mezquita Catedral de Córdoba*" (Mosque-Cathedral of Córdoba), a world's jewel of art and history, which was shown to us by a true expert—Manuel's daughter-in-law. A one-hour horse carriage historical tour with our granddaughter...*wow!* While in Córdoba, I toured the truly impressive manufacturing plant of "La Abuela Carmen." Nina got her introduction to my business life, and we took a marvelous picture with some of the executives of the company.

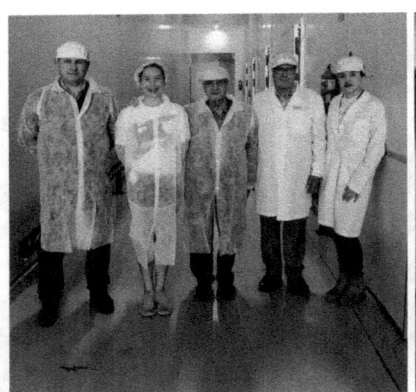 

Left: Salvador Sanchez, executive from "La Abuela Carmen," my granddaughter Nina, me, and the production and quality control managers. **Right:** My sister Mela, with her daughter Nenuca and granddaughters Susana and Cris on a beautiful street in Seville. Much of the city center's unique atmosphere is due to its Arabic influences and quaint narrow streets—too narrow for modern cars but almost narrow enough for neighbors on opposite sides of the street to shake hands!

From Córdoba, we continued our beautiful journey on the luxurious AVE bullet train to Seville. Seville is a unique type of city—an old city with Arabic influence, where all the flamenco music and dancing are an integral part of the city. It is a must-see for visitors! Bea and I stayed in a hotel, while our granddaughter Nina stayed for a few days with her third cousins—girls of her same age and with the same heritage: Luis Rugarcia's daughters who, like Nina, are the great-great-granddaughters of my grandfather, Casimiro Rugarcía. I am not sure how many families are able to trace their lineage and are still in touch with their third cousins, but I think it is wonderful, and I hope their connection continues. (Curiously enough, Luis' family will be the last Rugarcía descendants of my abuelo Casimiro, as Luis is the only great-grandson.)

A picture of the group in Seville: **Back row:** Luis' wife, Blanca, Bea, me, and Luis, **Front row:** Nina (seated), with Luis' daughters, Isabel, Maria, and Blanca Rugarcía

After the great vacation in Seville, we returned to Madrid for the life-changing taped interview with chess historian/journalist Miguel Angel Nepomuceno, an emotional visit with Juanjo de la Cierva, and a final dinner with the Madrid family. A chess-business-family vacation that I will never forget!

CHAPTER 13:
Miguel Angel Nepomuceno

We all have years of transition in our lives, and for me, 2017 was one such year. Meeting Miguel was an extraordinary coincidence, and the bond between us was a unique experience based on the incredible life passions and friendships that we shared. For one thing, he inspired me to become a writer. (Appendix B references a selection of the articles on chess I wrote after we met.) Miguel also felt very strongly that my father's life and family story had to be shared, and so I have, in this book.

As my memory flies back to that incredible decade of the 1940s, in Gijón and Madrid in my native Spain, there are also special memories of my departure for Cuba, in 1947. That year was a very special one for me. I had just finished my first year of medical school at Madrid University and was enjoying a long summer in Gijón. I was invited to play in the IV International Chess Tournament of Gijón, one of the highlights of my chess life. I ended up tied with Arturito Pomar and defeated the then-champion of Spain, I.M. Antonio Medina. Coincidentally, that was also the year when Miguel Angel was born—on the day of my nineteenth birthday.

It must have been the first week of September 1947, and I was ready to return to Madrid when I got some good news from my dear friend, Pablo ("Pablito") Morán. He had been invited to live with his uncle in Madrid so that he could develop what became a brilliant career in journalism, and he was excited about us both being in Madrid! Unfortunately, by coincidences of life, I had just learned that I would be leaving Spain for Cuba in November as the next step toward our family reunion. (It had been eleven years since the sad July 18, 1936, that had torn our family apart.)

On the day of my nineteenth birthday, the day that Miguel was born (give or take a week), Pablito Morán and I were again walking on the street and talking about chess. This time, however, we were not on the streets of Gijón, but in Madrid, walking from my home to the Maudes Chess Club. I was ready to introduce Pablo to all my dear friends as my replacement since I was about to leave for Cuba…where, ironically, Pablo had been born.

While I initiated a new life in Cuba and the US (many years later), Pablo remained in Spain, where he eventually met Miguel. Later in life, the two men became good friends and Miguel came to "know" me through the eyes of Pablo, who had often spoken of me. In addition, Professor Juan Fernandez Rua (a family friend with whom I had played multiple games as a child), was a good friend of Miguel Angel, and at some point, they discussed what *Don* Juan (the honorific title I use for Professor Fernandez Rua) remembered of his playing against me when I was a child.

From our extensive correspondence, one email in particular stands out, as it dealt with World Champion Alexander Alekhine, who had long been my idol. Miguel was one of the foremost Alekhine historians, and his knowledge about Alekhine's life is legendary. Since I was inspired by Alekhine's life lesson as a young kid, I remember with emotion what Miguel wrote to me on the subject:

"Dear Eugenio, before leaving for the hospital, I didn't want to forget to thank you for your words and add some other words by Alekhine that corroborate what he told you that day on the Calle Corrida when you were a youngster. It is, from a human standpoint, the best interview that Alekhine has ever given, besides being written by my dear friend Fernandez Rua, who told me so many things about "The Colossus." Alekhine, in July of 1944, said:

"The best part of my life occurred between two world wars that devastated Europe. They both ruined me, but with one difference: At the end of the first, I was twenty-six years old and had an unbridled enthusiasm that I no longer possess. If I someday write my memoirs (which is

very possible), people will find out that chess was a secondary factor in my life. It allowed me to hold onto and pursue an ambition, while at the same time, convincing me of the futility of ambition. Nowadays, I continue to play chess because it keeps my mind occupied and keeps me away from the obsessions and memories."

Miguel Angel Nepomuceno contacted me late in 2016 to ask me for an interview. We agreed to meet in Madrid on April 5th, 2017, as I was planning a "business-vacation" trip with my wife and my California granddaughter Nina. Miguel was interested in an interview for a series of articles in his chess column at the prestigious web magazine *"Zenda/ libros."*

I could not understand how a giant of journalism in Spain such as him could have an interest in someone who was a perfect unknown in the firmament of chess stars around the world. It turns out that he had read about my father and my book, *40 Years of Friendship, 100 Games of Chess* (2014), and he knew the story of my interaction with Alekhine.

We met at the Petit Palace Hotel in Madrid, across the street from the Retiro Park of my infancy. (He was almost seventy years old, and I was exactly nineteen years his senior.). After a lengthy conversation comparing notes, we had a three-hour-long taped interview, followed by many phone conversations and emails, which resulted in his five wonderful articles in *Zenda/libros.*

As soon as we started talking, I realized the origin of his interest— my family's story and the inspiring figure of my father, as well as the influence of Alekhine in my life. Miguel, while best known for his writings about music and about chess, was proud of his deep knowledge of the history of the Spanish Civil War. He inspired me to write about chess and especially about my family—he insisted that it was a story that had to be shared. When I asked him, "Seriously, then why don't we start with my father's story?" he replied with a broad smile and said that "he needed to make me famous first."

His articles indeed made me well-known in the world of Spanish chess. Here I was, an unknown figure from the 1940s who had interacted with and played against World Champion Alekhine and the Spanish champions Pomar, Toran, F.J. Perez, and Medina, with favorable results.

This April 2017 meeting was the start of a deep friendship. The emotional impact of my first and only personal meeting with Miguel is difficult to describe. It was like reliving my unforgettable years of the 1940s in Gijón and Madrid. (After all, *"Recordar es volver a vivir"*—to remember is to relive.) It felt as if the spirits of my father, Alekhine, and his historian Pablo Morán were somewhere, smiling while listening to our conversation. To make a real friendship at age eighty-nine defies conventional wisdom but is still believable. Telling people that there were spirits present overseeing and inspiring the conversation may sound silly to those who have never experienced something similar. Whether you believe it or not is entirely up to you.

While discussing my memories and what I told him about the Spanish Civil War in relation to Spanish philosopher Ortega y Gasset's assertion, "Man is himself plus his circumstances," Miguel replied to me: "Your memories are my circumstances—thanks to them, I have learned so much that I never knew." It was really something unique, a sort of revelation that began to appear before us when, while chatting, we realized we shared the same birthday, the same passion for chess, and our common friendship with Pablo Morán. There were also several other extraordinary parallels between our lives: our love for Asturias, starting (but never finishing) a degree in medicine, and our shared love of literature and music—the volume of serendipitous coincidences is almost too incredible to be believed.

Although it was our first meeting, Miguel Angel autographed his out-of-print book on Lasker for me and captured the depth of our connection with his use of the Spanish word *"reencontrado"*—a re-encounter, as if we had met before, which is exactly how it felt. In our initial discussion, I remembered (and told Miguel) that Pablito had, in a way, introduced us four decades before: He had not only spoken to Miguel about me but also commented to me about him. It was either 1973 or 1975, and Beatrice and I were visiting Pablo and Elena at their quaint summer place at the beach in Estaño (near Gijón), and Pablo mentioned a wonderful, young, new chess player who had just become champion of Asturias. His name (difficult to forget) was Nepomuceno.

Chapter 13: Miguel Angel Nepomuceno

In the months following our April 2017 interview, Miguel honored me with a series of five biographical articles in his well-read column in the *Zenda/libros* web magazine, under the title "Eugenio Salomon Rugarcía: From Alekhine to Kasparov or How to Play Blindfolded on the Board of Life". I was quite touched and humbled by some of his compliments, descriptions, and especially how he referred to me here:

"The protagonist of this story is not a Grand Master, although has defeated some of them. He is not a professional player...Eugenio Salomon Rugarcía is an authentic self-made man..."

Miguel Angel, Bea, and I at the hotel the day we first met.

Another wonderful consequence of my meeting with Miguel was my subsequent friendship with his friend, Jesus Remis Fernandez, who honored me by dedicating his beautiful article about the Maudes Chess Club of Madrid to me. (The article was published a few years later on the website, "Historia del ajedrez español," in the *Articulos* section, under the author's name.[2]

In 2019, brothers Pedro and Luis Mendez Castedo had their book about the Gijón International Tournaments published in English by McFarland, a well-known publisher of chess books. I was able to contribute to their book with original photographs and felt honored when I was asked to write the Foreword to the English edition. I was also

---
2 http://www.historiadelajedrezespanol.es/articulos/remis/13.htm

Sweet Memories — Family, Friends, Chess, and Sugar

invited to join them for an interview by *El Comercio*, a leading Gijón newspaper. I not only witnessed the origin of the event itself in 1943, but I am also the last surviving participant of the 1947 tournament. (Unfortunately, Miguel was unable to attend due to health reasons but participated in a conference call, and we had a wonderful interview.) Recently, when I published my book, *Jugando en el tablero de la vida* (published by Chessy, with co-author Javier Cordero), Luis honored me by writing the prologue.

When, in 2018, Miguel started having health problems, he was still determined to finish the sixth and final installment in the series of articles at *Zenda* dealing with my sixty years in the US and asked me to help him. In one of our many, many emails about our lives, memories, and the final article for *Zenda*, he had asked me to provide more details about my life in the 1960s and 1970s. I wrote about the first few years in Brooklyn, my work promotion, the family's move to New Jersey, my return to chess in the New Jersey Open after a sixteen-year-hiatus and joining the Westfield NJ Chess Club.

I also told him about having been one of the founding members of the club at Windows on the World in the early '70s, a restaurant open to the public at night but a private club during the day. It was located on the 107th floor of the World Trade Center. I had witnessed the construction of the Twin Towers for years during my daily commute to Wall Street. Tragically, on my way to a business meeting the morning of 9/11/2001, I watched those same towers collapse.

Aside from the horrific tragedy of 9/11, Miguel thought my stories were "magnificent" and told me, "I will put [these anecdotes] in order and adjust them, and it will be stupendous… your daily life. Yes, there is stupendous chess, but there are not always anecdotes like your story of the World Trade Center—even though it is [more than] thirty years old, it still belongs here."

Sadly, Miguel passed away in 2022. It was a rare privilege to have shared the writing of the last chapter with him, and I still hope to complete and publish it in his honor, for all that he has honored me.

CHAPTER 14:
Lifelong Friendships

Life without good friends must be difficult. When I left Cuba in 1960, I left behind my small farm, my car, and my savings, but fortunately, I did not lose the most important thing: my friends. As I write these lines, I feel in my soul the vacuum left by friends that have departed this world ahead of me. Because friends and friendship are such a central part of my life, I will dedicate this chapter to them.

Good friends have been one of the most precious experiences in my life. While thinking about friendships, at age ninety-four, when regretfully, one has lost so many...it goes without saying that I truly miss them! Some were made during my youth in Spain and my university days in Cuba, some were made over the board in chess, and some were made during my seventy-five-year career in the sugar industry. My chess friends are discussed in my chess writings, so I will focus now on those friends from my days in Spain and Cuba, with emphasis on the number of bilingual friends with whom I have maintained a lifelong close relationship.

Childhood and school friends

Aside from Alvarín (my first friend who I lost much too soon when a grenade exploded in his hands), I have beautiful memories of two childhood friendships: Luis Fernandez Renau (my neighbor in Madrid), with whom I had the pleasure of reuniting in New York and in Madrid fifty and seventy years later; and Paco Luis Alvarez (my friend from Gijón during the Civil War), who later emigrated to Colombia. Paco

Luis and I met up several decades later in Madrid when we were both on vacation with our wives.

I must also mention two unforgettable high school friends with whom I have had continued contact for decades: Manolín Gonzalez Rico, my friend from the "*Instituto Jovellanos*" in Gijón (with whom I would meet whenever I visited Spain), and Antonio Ruiz San Miguel from the *Ramiro de Maeztu* High School in Madrid, with whose family I remain in contact. Wherever their spirits are today, I am sure they will hear my message of memories…and gratitude.

During my last sixty-two years of life, in this "good old USA," I was blessed with a new set of friends—a large, diverse group that included my wife's cousins and our neighbors. For the purposes of this chapter, I will only focus on the remarkable group that I will call my "Bilingual friends."

Bilingual friends

I found it curious to observe that for the last sixty-plus years, I had a group of close friends with whom I shared a surprisingly deep "bilingual friendship." It is not until now, while writing about my friendships, that I suddenly realized the profound influence of a bilingual culture on friendships. For reasons too long to explain, sharing a dual language creates some invisible bond. There is much more to language than simple communication—I believe there is a psychological component that creates instant understanding. It is not by coincidence that about half of my dozen closest friends, whether born in Spain or Cuba, also came to the US after the Cuban Revolution. Since my business activities involved a lot of travel to Europe and the Caribbean, I was privileged to be able to maintain personal contact with them over the years.

Here are a few examples of dear friends with whom I shared roots from Spain and/or Cuba, including the voluntary emigration from both places, and the continuation of a great friendship.

Chapter 14: Lifelong Friendships

The Zulueta family

I am proud to say that I have been friends with three generations of the Zulueta family. It began in Havana with Julian Zulueta (sugar mill owner and founder of the *Banco Continental Cubano*) who contracted me as the teacher/preceptor for his older sons, Fernando and Javier, in November 1947. Years after being their tutor, we three became friends and enjoyed many years of friendship, which has now been extended to my whole family.

The family friendship continues today with Julian's grandchildren. One of his grandsons, Javi Zulueta, and his wife, Maite, celebrated the 2021 Thanksgiving in New York with our family shortly after he joined the staff of the prestigious Mt. Sinai Hospital in New York as a medical researcher and professor.

Celebrating 2021 Thanksgiving Day in Manhattan: Javi and Maite Zulueta are the couple at the far left.

We have maintained a lifelong family friendship from Havana to Philadelphia to Madrid and back to New York…including visits/vacations in San Sebastian and Santander in Spain, or in New York and Miami in the US.

Juan Jose de la Cierva

Juan Jose "Juanjo" de la Cierva was an engineer and a *concuñado* (brother-in-law) of Javier Zulueta, and we became good friends when he arrived in Cuba from Spain in 1952. He was also the first Spaniard to win an Oscar award for Best Technical Film Contribution (1970). He had invented the Dynalens, an image stabilizer used largely by the US Army for aerial filming, which the film industry later adapted for moviemaking. (He owned more than fifty patents.)

At one point in the 1960s, Juan Jose invited me to travel to Pompano Beach, Florida. A racetrack there had just installed his invention "instant photo finish," which he had patented in Spain many years before. I went, and we had a wonderful time. Years later, when he had some business problems in Spain, he asked me to keep a box with all his patents at my home in New Jersey where they would be secure, far from Spain. Yes, we had a lot of interactions, including his offer that I become the chairman of his successful Philadelphia company...the only time I refused (fortunately) an offer from my good friend!

On one of his trips returning to Spain, during a stopover in NY, Juanjo called me to see if we could get together. The only time we could meet was the night when I had a formal (tuxedo) banquet at the Waldorf Astoria for the annual Sugar Industry dinner. It was our only chance to see each other, so I invited him to our table...where he was the only one at the gala dinner not wearing a tuxedo. During the dinner, he told his new friends: "Delighted to meet you. Last week I was sitting at another remarkable table..." That had been the Oscar Award ceremony, and big Hollywood stars (including Elizabeth Taylor) were seated at his table.

The last (but not least) of our coincidental visits took place during my memorable vacation in Spain in 2017. Right after my unforgettable interview with Miguel Angel Nepomuceno (on the morning of April 5th), I visited with Juanjo and his brother-in-law at the same hotel. It was the last time we would see each other, a farewell to a long, bilingual friendship covering the same itinerary: Spain to Cuba to the US, followed by multiple meetings in both Spain and the U.S.

Chapter 14: Lifelong Friendships

Manuel Hernández Fumero

Manuel "Manolito" Hernandez Fumero was a fellow engineering student in Havana and my partner in our farm and trucking business in Cuba. (I still maintain a close relationship with his son, Pablo Manuel, my godchild, who lives in Puerto Rico.) In 1959, while my parents were living with me in Havana, my father asked me to plant a tree in his name in a corner of the farm that "Manolito" and I had bought in *La Salud,* an agricultural area in the outskirts of Havana. (I did but never got to see it grow.) In the 1980s, I had the opportunity to spend a few days with Manolito's family on their houseboat in Isabela, Puerto Rico—that unique place of phosphorescent fish!! Then I had the privilege of having my godson drive me around the entire island—the best tour guide I ever had!!

Julio Bordas Alonso

Julio Bordas Alonso was my close friend in agricultural engineering—I traveled 800 km from Havana to Bayamo by bus to be a witness at his wedding! He became a well-known painter in exile. In this picture, Bea is sitting under a beautiful landscape of his dear Bayamo. He is living in Miami and is the only one of the friends from my Havana University days who is still alive.

"Paco Prima" (Francisco Lopez Macias)

Paco was also born in Spain, and his family left for Cuba when the Spanish Civil War started. We first met in 1948 at the ACU and became instant friends. Because there was already another Paco in the ACU, he was known as "Paco Prima," and everyone called him that.

I remember one time he lent me his algebra book, which I took to my exam but accidentally left the book in the classroom afterward. The assistant came out to announce that someone had forgotten their book, calling out, "Francisco Lopez Macias… Francisco Lopez Macias…" I rolled my eyes, wondering who could possibly have forgotten their book? Since no one ever called him by his real name, it did not even occur to me that the book was Paco's, and the stupid guy who forgot it was me. We had a good laugh about it later.

Paco and I remained in close contact after his wedding in Cuba. A few years later, they settled in New Orleans (which I visited two to three times a year on business), and later moved to Santo Domingo, where we were able to meet every year. Our families remained close for the rest of Paco's life, and we are still in close contact with his children. His son, who just died recently, was also my godchild, and I played (and beat) one of his daughters, "Mamusa," in a game of blindfolded chess at their home in Santo Domingo. Another of Paco's daughters, "Lula," is very close to my children. (We socialized frequently while she was living in New York.) It makes me smile to remember that this grown woman, now an author, was the little girl her father and I once picked up from school in New Orleans during one of my many visits with them during the late-1960s.

Lula has converted the deep and beautiful stories of her life experiences as a bilingual child of immigrants into a longitudinal children's book and video series entitled: *MariVi the Master Navigator*. Thousands, if not millions of bilingual immigrant children will recognize their story in the first book of the series, entitled *School Crossing*.

Ceferino "Fino" Cata

"Fino" was a medical student when I entered Havana University Agricultural and Sugar Engineering School in 1948. Soon after we met, I learned about his Spanish roots. Although he was born in Palma Soriano, Cuba, in 1926, the first memories of his life were of the one year he spent in his father's native Spain at age five. Fino was a classmate of Fidel Castro at the Dolores Jesuit School in Santiago de Cuba and became a successful medical doctor in Havana. After taking his medical exams in the US, he relocated to Dayton, Ohio, with his family. We saw each other almost yearly when he visited his sister in NJ, and we remained close friends. On one occasion, Fino and Maria Elena spent a couple of days' vacation at our New Jersey home.

Sixty years of friendship— Paco Prima, Ceferino Cata, and myself

Dr. Ceferino Cata (and his wife, Maria Elena), Paco Prima (and his wife, Beba), Bea, and I continued the friendship born in 1948 in Havana for life in the US. In 2008, we decided to take a vacation together to Miami to celebrate the sixty-year anniversary of our friendship. We decided not to stay with friends or relatives but to be together in a hotel. We organized a Spanish luncheon visit with Father Llorente from the ACU and were invited to a "Cuban friends" evening party organized by other mutual friends.

These bilingual friends mean the world to me and are always in my heart.

In life, we all make deeper friendships when we share common backgrounds. Whether you are a musician, writer, chess player, or sugar man, obviously, those activities are the basis for good friendships. Although this chapter did not focus on my friends from the sugar industry, many of them share the same background and Cuban life experience as me. I remember them fondly as well.

Left: L-R: Dr. "Fino" Cata, Maria Elena, Beatrice Salomon, "Beba," and "Paco Prima" Lopez Macias. (I was the photographer.) Bea and I continue to stay in touch with Maria Elena and Beba. **Right**: Paco Prima and Julio Bordas in Miami 2008, celebrating sixty years of friendship (Julio is the only close friend from my ACU days who is still alive).

CHAPTER 15:
Our Family Tree and Family Ties

As important as chess was in my life, it would always take a backseat to family. Family was a priority for my father, and he never missed an opportunity to spend time with relatives. He also made sure his children understood how important it was to remain connected, which is why (and how) I have been able to retain contact with so many family members worldwide.

I was fortunate to have met a few of my father's first cousins while he was alive, and while researching this book, I had wonderful conversations with many of them. It was truly a pleasure reminiscing with them, and several surprised me with stories and photos I had never seen or heard!

Meeting some of my father's cousins

It must have been March or April of 1959, while the Cuban Revolution was still popular in Cuba, when my father told me that a dear cousin of his, Dr. Rudy Joseph, and his wife, Mildred, were coming to Havana from Miami on a cruise vacation. My father told me Rudy had completed his medical school studies in Italy to escape Hitler's madness and then had come to the US, where he became a successful MD in Long Island, New York. We met them at the ship and showed them around town. I never suspected that sixty-two years later, I would be writing about that meeting. My family and the Joseph family have remained close ever since.

Rudy Joseph was the first of my father's first cousins that I had ever met. He had been born in Germany, and his family was Jewish. Some years ago, Rudy was the subject of a three-part video interview about his life experiences. The footnote contains the links to the three videotaped interviews that he gave to a journalist. [3]

Left: Partial family picture, taken in 1993, near the date of my son Henry's wedding. Standing: Rudy Joseph; myself; my son Robbie; my son Gene Jr.; my wife, Bea; sister Mela's husband, Guillermo; Seated: my sister Mela, Mildred Joseph. **Right:** A treasured picture of Rudy Joseph and his son, Peter, with some of the tools of their shared profession—medicine

The second of my father's cousins I met was Frank Sanders. Late in 1959 (or early in 1960, before the sugar mills were expropriated by Castro), I was an executive in the sugar industry in Cuba and had to travel to Battle Creek, Michigan, to visit our largest US client, the cereal company Kellogg's. Since I was supposed to fly from Havana to New York, my father urged me to visit another of his first cousins, Frank Sanders (also a survivor of Hitler), who had become a successful lawyer in Manhattan specializing in recovering items confiscated by the Nazis. Frank had been born with the last name Salomon but had changed his name to Sanders when starting a new life in the US. He and his wife, Lola, lived on Cabrini Blvd near that little-known jewel, The Cloisters, in the Washington Heights section of Manhattan, which was a German-Jewish neighborhood at that time. I remember visiting their home and being amazed to learn for the first time that Frank used to visit our home in Madrid and listen to classical music quartets on

---

3 Part 1: https://www.dropbox.com/s/6f05rz84lq2s3w2/VTS_02_1.VOB?dl=0
Part 2: https://www.dropbox.com/s/dr9ooae5emgncuv/VTS_02_2.VOB?dl=0
Part 3: https://www.dropbox.com/s/4hv3k95oabmycnq/VTS_02_3.VOB?dl=0

weekends, while my mother was expecting her last child—myself! It was obviously an emotional reunion—Frank and my father had been very close. My father had been Frank's mentor at the German company AEG (where my father had a high management position) when Frank came to Madrid to work as a management trainee.

Frank was even able to recover a *"Silberner Löffel Stander"* (silver spoon holder), which had been confiscated by the Nazis from his parents' home. It had been crafted by a famous German artist and was on exhibition at a German museum. Having no children, Frank donated the beautiful piece to me before he passed away. Years later, I gifted that family treasure to my granddaughter, Sophie, on the occasion of her *bat mitzvah*, the Jewish coming-of-age ceremony. I felt it was poetic justice—a Salomon was returning to the family's Jewish roots, and it was fitting that she should have it.

In 1988, when Frank learned that I was hoping to write a family book with my father's memoirs, he also gave me a lot of information that he had developed about the family genealogy. According to Frank, my great-great grandfather, Moses Salomon, was born in 1795 in Horsheim a/Rhein and is buried at the Jewish cemetery in the village of Weitersburg, near Vallendar (in the Alsace region), which Frank had visited.

Moses' wife, Lina Danzig (my great-great-grandmother), had a brother who came to the US around 1848, worked at Sutro Brothers, and later became one of the governors of the New York Stock Exchange. Frank told me that a picture of him and his wife was still hanging on the wall of the Jewish Home for the Aged at West 106th St. in Manhattan.

In 1962, when my brother came to the Sloan Kettering Hospital in Manhattan for a last effort to save his life, my parents flew in from Madrid and stayed with us in New York, so that they could be with Roberto if circumstances permitted. During the couple of weeks that my parents were with us in Brooklyn, my father managed to introduce me to another set of first cousins, Liesel, Lotti, and Ella Schwarz (my father's first cousins), who had left Germany and relocated to Queens, NY. They had a brother, Ernst, who lived in Portland, Oregon, whom

I met years later at a family reunion. Ernst had two sons, Jerry and Maurice, with whom we maintained a lifelong family contact.

As I am typing this page, something funny happened. I had called my second cousin, Jerry Schwarz, in Boston (a retired professor at Brandeis University) to double-check my memory of names and relationships. After our conversation, as I started to type again, the phone rang.... It was another Schwarz cousin—Annette Wolff from Montreal—about whom I had just commented with Jerry. Should I chalk that up to ESP, or should I just add it to the list of my ninety-four years of coincidences?

I met the final set of my father's cousins in 1963, while in London for a business meeting. When my father in Madrid learned about my trip, he sent me the address of his very dear first cousin, John Woolf, and asked me not to miss visiting him. John had been born Hans Wolff in Germany and had been lucky enough to escape Hitler's madness. Hans was my father's first cousin on his mother's side (Schwarz) and was the nephew of my "Grossmama," Anna Schwarz, who had lived with us in Madrid in the early 1930s. I met Hans at his home on the outskirts of London some sixty years ago, which was the beginning of a great family relationship. (His daughter, Annette, was either away in college or working at the NATO headquarters in Brussels.)

While drafting this book and contacting all my family with questions, I learned a great deal about Hans' mother, Helene (the younger sister of my Grossmama), who tragically died of starvation in the Theresienstadt Nazi concentration camp.

When I contacted Annette Woolf (who now lives in Montreal), and we started to compare notes, a new world opened to me: Annette's grandmother, Helene Schwarz, and my grandmother, Anna Schwarz, were sisters! Helene, still living in Germany under Hitler, was much younger than her sister Anna, and my grandmother was living with us in Madrid in the early 1930s. Both sisters kept a lot of their correspondence. Unbeknownst to me, it turns out that Annette's grandmother was our "*Tia Elena*"—the "Aunt Helene" who kept the pictures of my sisters, brother, and myself that my proud *Grossmama* sent to her; hence, the "Dear Aunt Helene" salutation. I never knew this—or perhaps I just did not realize the connection.

Left: Wedding picture of Heinrich and Helene Wolff (née Schwarz), June 12, 1894. **Center:** My siblings' First Holy Communion announcement sent by Grossmama to her sister, Helene (Tia Elena); **Right:** Helene Wolff, September 1940, living in the Judenhaus at 26A Emserstrasse.

Annette found this postcard from Tia Elena, sent shortly before the family was informed of her death. As I learned this, my stomach got a funny feeling: Before that moment, I never knew how close my life had been to the Holocaust—just one degree of separation. I will always remember this tragic story of the love of these two sisters.

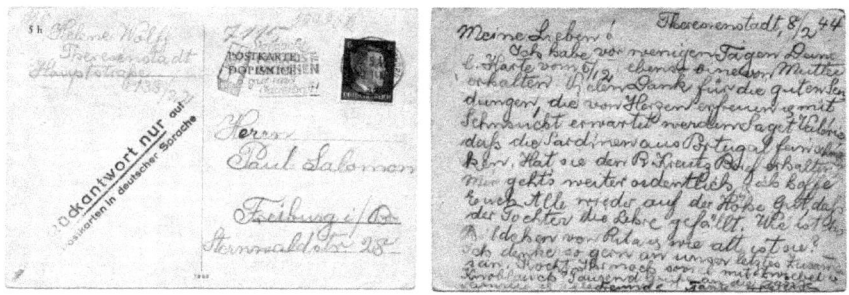

Helene's last postcard from Theresienstadt to her nephew Paul Salomon, dated February 8, 1944, about one and a half months before her death.

Sweet Memories — Family, Friends, Chess, and Sugar

My reunion with Uncle Max's family

The reader already knows the history of the families of Max and Robert Salomon and the estrangement that arose between them due to their political differences. The two brothers reunited at the last minute when my father flew to Mexico as brother Max was in his final days.

During the 1960s, I had to travel to Mexico on business. On one of my first trips, I tried to follow my father's example to heal old wounds. My father indicated that I should go to the Amsterdam Jewelry Store in Mexico City and ask for Juanchu.

The jewelry store employee looked surprised, and she told me she did not know anyone by that name. Seated nearby, there was an older man who, upon hearing the conversation, looked up and said to me, "Yes, in the family and in Spain, you all know him as Juanchu. Here we all call him German." That man was the father of Felix Hernández Molina, author of a book about the times his father and my Uncle Max shared titled, *Letters from a German*. That is how I was able to reconnect with my cousin Juanchu, who I had not seen since before the start of the Spanish Civil War in 1936.

Left: German "Juanchu" and his wife, Lilly; **Right**: Danny, Lilly, Ricardo, Regina, and Juanchu

The same invisible walls that my father, Robert, broke down when he reunited with his brother, Max, fell again that day. (In life, almost every problem has a solution—sometimes, you just must look for it.) That unity has remained intact over the years and has included family reunions in Mexico, New York, Los Angeles, and Madrid. After two or three visits with Juanchu, Lilly, and their children (Ricardo, Regina, and Dany), Juanchu asked me if I would like to visit his mom, my *Tía*

Concha. I clearly did not remember her since I had not seen her since I was too young to remember, but it was still emotional. I was sure that she, like my mother, had been the anonymous "heroine" raising the children under the most difficult circumstances. Tia Concha was the sister of the "*hermanos Cazalis*," (Cazalis brothers), Jai-Alai world champions at one point. (The traditionally Basque sport of jai-alai was popular in Cuba). By coincidences of life, I had met both Cazalis brothers at the *frontón* (jai alai arena) in Havana where they were working as agents taking bets.

Contacts with Uncle Paul's family

The oldest of the three brothers was Uncle Paul. He and his son Lothar had visited us in Madrid around 1932, when Grossmama was living with us. (I do not remember them as I was only three or four years old.) When Uncle Paul (whose wife was a Christian) decided to stay in Metz for the duration of the war, he decided at the same time to make sure he would save the lives of his two children, Hedwig and Lothar, and sent them to stay with close friends in Australia.

Over the years, my sister Ana Maria, "the family ambassador," kept in touch with the entire family, even with Uncle Paul who, with the help of friends, was able to survive in Hitler-occupied France. Not too many years ago, Lothar visited Ana Maria in Madrid, and they called me on the phone. It was a pleasant surprise to talk with him. I had had some "old-fashioned" letter correspondence with him back in 1999, but had not seen him since Madrid, 1932.

When my son Robbie got married in 2001, he and his wife visited Sydney, Australia, on their honeymoon. Like my father used to do with me, I urged my son to visit his cousin Lothar (Paul's son) in Australia, which he did! One of Lothar's sons, Dr. Ralph Salmon, is a physician in Oxford, UK. The other son, Grant, lives in New Zealand.

Dr. Carmen Moriyon Salomon, my father's granddaughter (and sister Mela's daughter) from Madrid, had contacted Ralph in England some years ago, and another family connection was born. Years later, when my son Robbie was on sabbatical from NYU and spending one year in Madrid, Bea and I went on vacation to visit them and all the family. By sheer coincidence, Ralph was also on vacation in Madrid. Robbie and I were fortunate to be able to share bread and family stories with him.

The 1999 reunion

When my sister Ana Maria was planning a vacation with us in 1999, a distant cousin from Buenos Aires (Vivian Salomon, whom I had met through my father in 1962 as a law student at NYU) advised me that she was planning a vacation to New York. (Thirty-seven years later, she would help me to complete the genealogical tree with first-hand information about the Argentinian branch of the Salomon family tree.) As a lucky coincidence, she would be visiting while my sister was here, so I decided to organize a family reunion in New Jersey. Juanchu and Lilly came from Mexico, and so did my father's first cousins from New York (Dr. Rudy, Mildred Joseph, and their children Peter and Jane), as well as Cousin Vivian (then from Buenos Aires) with her husband, Carlos (from Croatia, then Yugoslavia), and their son Diego.

In total, there were thirty people with Salomon relatives from four different countries. Differences of religion and political ideas were set aside, and we all enjoyed a reunion where we shared family warmth and solidarity. It was truly a tribute to my father's life.

Chapter 15: Our Family Tree and Family Ties

Back row, L-R: sister Ana Maria; daughter-in-law Anna; daughter-in-law Danielle; son Gene; wife, Bea; Diego (Vivian Salomon's son); Jane Joseph's husband, David; son-in-law Mike; daughter Maria; Jane Joseph; Peter Joseph's wife, Marcia; Peter Joseph; Mildred Joseph; Carlos (Vivian Salomon's husband); Dr. Rudy Joseph; cousins Juanchu and Lilly
Kneeling, L-R: son Robbie, daughter-in-law (then fiancé) Julie, brother-in-law Jose, son Henry with grandson Matt in his arms, myself, my granddaughter Jessica, and a granddaughter of Rudy and Mildred also named Jessica

Villa Almendares poem

On my mother's side, it has been 110 years since Abuelito (my grandfather Casimiro) bought that small piece of heaven that he called "Villa Almendares". A century has passed since my cousins (the Menendez Rugarcía) played in the "*finca de Mareo.*" But neither the unstoppable advance of time nor the separations that occurred could make us forget those days. Decades later, my cousin Chuqui (one of the amazing young women who mothered me during the Spanish Civil War) authored a beautiful poem dedicated to Villa Almendares, in which she beautifully describes the "heaven on earth" that our family enjoyed, as well as the adversities and difficult times they endured:

Sweet Memories — Family, Friends, Chess, and Sugar

It stands out against the sky, visible from afar
As grand as a palace, was the house of Rugarcía.
Containing a marvelous park with a grotto and a fountain
Its leafy, green forest always offering shade and freshness
There grew the araucarias (monkey puzzle trees) along with the chestnut, thorn bushes,
eucalyptus and acacia, banana, lime, and lemon trees…
Round, fat groves of holm oak, cedar, and walnut
Some with byzantine domes, others like cathedral spires.
Over the door there was a sign that read "Villa Almendares"
More appropriate and more truthful would have been "Burdens lifted here."
Then there were the inhabitants, slightly artistic and eccentric
A family of dreamers who did not feel the passing of the years.
Reunited here, always content, we passed many happy hours
But only in fairy tales does bliss take root and last.
Of all that, nothing remains, only the memory, like a story.
The family was dispersed like the leaves taken by the wind.
Death took the elders, those who remained went traveling
Wandering through life with little luck, but they continue to dream.
They have ardent faith and calm souls,
those of the house of Rugarcía.
—Gijón 1962

The "Cantolla story"

It was early in 2007, and I was helping Luis Rugarcía (son of my youngest first cousin, Miguel Rugarcía) with some information for a family history project. During one phone conversation, Luis mentioned a sensational book from a dear friend of his grandfather's, Miguel Angel Diaz (known as "Cantolla"). Cantolla had just published his autobiography under the title *Entre los Picos de Europa*, an enjoyable book about his life and his love for those beautiful mountains in Northern Spain. He apparently had a strong friendship with my father—something I did not know years ago but discovered in 2007 while reading his autobiography. In the book, he refers to my father as his "Grandfather Salomón" and mentions my uncle and godfather Eugenio Rugarcía, referring to him as his "uncle and *padrino*." He even described how, with my father's help, he opened his own wristwatch business in the mountains.

Back then, I did not know who Cantolla was, and I was very confused—how could it be that he was so close with my father, and I didn't know anything about him? When I finished the book, I was able to find his phone number (by looking up his wristwatch business), and I decided to call him. The conversation went like this:

"Cantolla?" I asked when he answered the phone.

"Yes, who is this?"

"I am calling from the United States. I just read your book and wanted to congratulate you—it is wonderful."

"Okay, fine—but who is this?"

"Well, my name is Eugene Salomon, the son of your 'Grandfather Roberto' and nephew of your 'Uncle Eugenio,' so I am not sure whether I am your father or your brother."

We laughed heartily, and after speaking for some time, we determined that his words about my uncle had been accurate. In Spanish, the term "*padrino*" can mean either godfather at birth or best man at one's wedding; my Uncle Eugenio, who was my baptismal godfather, had also been the best man at Cantolla's wedding, so he was indeed *padrino* to both of us. We agreed that we needed to meet, and he offered to bring me to the Picos de Europa so I could see the majestic places where he had brought my father to relive the excursions of his youth. The offer from Cantolla was too exciting to pass up.

This was the origin of my desire to celebrate my eightieth birthday the following year in Spain, visiting the places that were so meaningful in the life of my father.

We agreed to meet in Potes (his hometown near the *Picos*) after the

September 29th, 2008, family dinner to celebrate my eightieth birthday. I wanted to be with my family in the Madrid of my memories. (To make it more "palatable" to my children and grandchildren, I promised them that for my eightieth, we would have two celebrations—one in Madrid, and another for Thanksgiving weekend at a resort area in Florida. They happily agreed.)

After we met in person, Cantolla autographed his last book for me: *Liebana, un paraíso en la Tierra* (*Liebana, Paradise on Earth*), addressing me as "Dear Brother Eugenio" ...and I know he meant it!

That same year, in October, my grand-nephew Robertín Moriyon, who I watched grow up during the years that his parents were at Princeton University for his father Roberto's doctorate in mathematics, was getting married in Oviedo, Spain, not far from Potes. We quickly arranged a trip to celebrate my birthday, attend the wedding, and spend a few days with Cantolla visiting the places that had fascinated my father during his youth.

My eightieth birthday

Before traveling to northern Spain in 2008, we spent several days in Madrid. There, I attended a dinner celebrating my eightieth birthday with my Spanish family. You cannot imagine my surprise when my four children showed up in the restaurant—I was overcome with emotion. They had come from Los Angeles, New York, and New Jersey to be with their father in Madrid. (Not even my wife, Bea, knew they were coming!) As a gift, my sister, Mela, painted an oil portrait for me, and my niece María Cristina, whom I had seen born in Cuba,

The ruins of an old castle and an old village in the Picos de Europa, taken by me during the trip with Cantolla.

brought me an album full of photos on behalf of the whole family. I admit without shame that I cried tears of joy.

The Picos de Europa mountains

The following day, we went to Potes so I could meet Miguel Ángel "Cantolla" in person. He drove us to several spots in the Picos de Europa. It was incredibly special to travel to the same beautiful, captivating spots my father had visited. Cantolla, always the gentleman, promised to bring us to Oviedo in his car to attend Robertín's wedding, and it was a pleasure accepting his offer.

Back to Spain…for bridge!

In 2011, my nephew, Rober, invited me to be his partner in an international bridge tournament to be played at the Gijón Yacht Club *Real Club Astur de Regatas*. There is only one thing I cannot resist in life: temptation! It was the same club where, more than sixty years earlier, I had played in the IV Gijón International Chess Tournament. It had also been the site of the high school graduation of the Class of 1946, where my childhood friends were graduating. I attended as an invited guest—had I not relocated to Madrid in 1943, that would have been my graduation as well.

A gift from the organizers of the bridge tournament, for traveling from New York to participate.

Sweet Memories — Family, Friends, Chess, and Sugar

From left to right: Cantolla; his wife, Lupe; my wife, Bea; my sister Mela; her son Rober; and myself.

Taking advantage of the trip to Gijón for the team bridge tournament, I contacted my new friend "Cantolla" again. I hoped that we could spend a pleasant evening dining at La Solana, a restaurant in Mareo situated on the former site of my grandfather's estate, Villa Almendares. We spent a lovely afternoon—myself, Bea, Cantolla and his wife, Lupe; my sister Mela, and my niece and nephews Espe and Robert.

More recent memories from Spain

In 2018, to honor Uncle Max for defending Madrid during the Spanish Civil War, there was an official ceremony to honor "the German Jew who saved Madrid," as the newspapers had dubbed him. The City Hall of the town where he fought dedicated the area to his name. In his memory, the name selected for the site was *"La Peña del Aleman"* (The Rock of the German). Family members from Spain, Mexico, and Canada who could attend the ceremony enjoyed a family reunion in Spain to honor Max's heroism. Despite past political differences, the bonds of blood prevailed.

Ana Maria turns one hundred

In 2021, my oldest sister Ana Maria turned one hundred. Sadly, due to Covid, we could not celebrate together as we wished. Instead, the family made her a special book of pictures and birthday wishes from around the world. Here are some extracts from that book:

Chapter 15: Our Family Tree and Family Ties

From me:

My dear sister,

We were four, but only you and I remain, the oldest and the youngest. Nine decades of family love shared from Spain and France to Cuba and Jamaica and the United States. We have so many memories, some sad and some beautiful, but most importantly, we have the family bonds full of the love we learned from our parents.

Porque tu vida fue rica y porque "recordar es volver a vivir" quiero celebrarla contigo con esta colección de recuerdos. Muchos besos de tu hermano, el "Benjamín."

From my wife, Bea:

Querida Ana Maria:

On your one-hundredth birthday, I wish you many more happy and healthy ones. I remember the time Gene and I spent with you in Jamaica. How well you received me to become another sister and then, over the years, the love you gave our family. With much love. —Beatrice

From my son Gene and his family:

Dear Tia Ani,

I'm very sorry we couldn't be with you to celebrate one hundred years of life. We wish you continued good health and many more years ahead. I hope we have an opportunity to get together again soon.

All our love, Gene, Danielle, Ella & Nina

From my son Henry to his godmother:

Querida Tía Ani:

Feliz cumpleaños número 100 de tu sobrino favorito. Podemos decir eso, porque no tenemos que decírselo a los demás. Espero que tengas un día maravilloso y que disfrutes con alguna tarta. Tengo muchos buenos recuerdos de Comillas.

Un abrazo muy fuerte desde Texas, Henry

From my daughter Maria:

A century young—honored that I got to spend fifty-eight of your one hundred years with you as my aunt. Happiest of birthdays—and just so you know, I'm the niece the devil gave to you. So many hugs and kisses to you. Hope to one day soon give them to you in person.

Love, Maria

From my son Robbie and his family:

Feliz cumpleaños hito Tía Ani. Wow, los 100!! Qué maravilla y qué vida bien vivida. Sentimos muchísimo no poder estar contigo para abrazarte, felicitarte, brindarte y celebrarte. Siempre recordaremos los tiempos que pasamos juntos en Madrid (comiendo en La Cafetería Bruselas) y Majadahonda (comiendo en El Cortijo),…y los veranos en Comillas y Torla. Esperamos verte pronto, pero mientras tanto, besos y abrazos con todo cariño!!

Robbie, Julie, Ben, y Sophie

Dearest Ani,

You are a beautiful inspiration to all who aspire to follow in your tracks. Much love on this happy achievement!

Peter and Marcy

Ana Maria, myself, and Mela at a restaurant in Madrid

Final thoughts

When we reach old age, we begin to ask some philosophical questions: Where did we come from, and where do we go? As for our memories—incredibly important to the life of each person—do they go somewhere at the end, or are they simply lost forever? More than once, I have thought that perhaps, when the spirit leaves our body, it takes all our memories with it, but who could ever know with any certainty? It has always been my goal to pass on my memories to those who might benefit from them; hence, this book.

I truly hope that younger readers, whether playing on the board of chess or the board of life, will always keep in mind that the important thing is to become a master of your own life. Whether your passion is chess, baseball, or music, enjoy it, but do not allow any passion to control your life. Instead, focus on promoting unity and respect for all people and cast aside extreme ideologies and hatred. I learned this from my father and from surviving multiple global conflicts and will continue to share that philosophy as long as I can. It is the only way to find peace.

A beautiful family Christmas celebration with my children and their families, New Jersey, circa 2014

EPILOGUE:
Sweet Reality & Sweet Dreams

As my ninety-fifth birthday approaches, a few remarkable things have happened in each sector of my life (family, friends, chess, and sugar) while we were finishing translating and adapting this book from Spanish to English.

I have heard it said that there is no happiness in life, but there are certainly happy moments. While working feverishly on editing my book of sweet memories, I was still privileged to live the even sweeter reality of enjoying family life, hoping that I had earned that privilege and that my grandchildren may be as lucky as I consider myself. This week, our daughter Maria drove us to a family dinner reunion in Manhattan to celebrate the graduation of our granddaughter Ella from New York University (NYU). Fortunately, three of our four children and four of our seven grandchildren were able to attend, and we were very pleased to also have Jane Joseph (daughter of my father's first cousin, the late Dr. Rudy Joseph) celebrate with us. I met Jane as a little girl back in 1960—family ties are wonderful!

The previous week, our son Robbie drove us several hours to visit our granddaughter Sophie in New Hampshire, a "freshwoman" at Dartmouth. When Robbie pointed out the library as a remarkable historical place on campus, I took a picture, and to my surprise, it highlighted 1928—the year of my birth! Laughing out loud, my son Robbie said, "Yes, Dad, one man's fact is another man's coincidence."

As my writing career comes to an end with this book, the May 2023 issue of the quarterly web magazine *The Chess Journalist* has published my final article, titled "From Alekhine to Kasparov and Beyond." At the same time, I am working with the club's president, my friend Nick Carlson, to schedule my "Farewell Lecture" at the Toms River Chess Club for September—the month of my ninety-fifth birthday. I was honored to be inducted into their Hall of Fame, along with several world champions and distinguished Grandmasters. When I last spoke there, at age ninety, I was told that I wasn't the oldest speaker they've had, since Edward Lasker gave a lecture at age ninety-two. I want to beat Lasker by three years!

Besides memories and realities, I still continue with my dreams. In 2017, during an unforgettable family vacation-business-chess trip to Spain, I had a business dream. After visiting the state-of-the-art Maillard reaction plant in Córdoba, Spain, that my friend and consulting client Manuel Vaquero Ortiz runs for the production of black garlic, I got an idea: Organic black garlic infused into organic molasses could be a sweetener of choice for Europe's consumers, who have a sweet tooth but are also health conscious. It took years of product and business development, but, in my dreams, I can visualize the first of several items in the European and Canadian retail stores, hopefully before my upcoming ninety-fifth birthday. Connecting my business friends from the 1960s meetings in Barbados with the new ones in Spain was a pleasure and will hopefully yield a first collaborative breakthrough soon.

Last but not least, Brian O'Malley, an old friend from the sugar industry and past president of the Domino Sugar group, approached me to seek my permission to nominate me for the Dyer Award "Sugar Man of the Year". In my mind, this is essentially the highest honor in the industry. I thought, *My God, how sweet it is to have your peers in the industry honor you!*

Even after eighty years—a lifetime—of chess, I never reached the level of "Grandmaster". In chess, only the best Grandmasters compete for the title of World Champion via the Candidates Matches. In my mind, the competition for the Sugar Man of the Year/Dyer Award is similar to the Candidates Matches. Since I was being nominated for what I would consider the World Champion title in the sugar industry, I like to think that simply being nominated made me a "Sugar

Grandmaster" (even though I know full well that I don't have the most remote chance of winning).

Because the main focus of the book is not just sugar, I know it might have been difficult to follow my industry career, which spanned sixty years. For this reason, I have included an appendix called "How I Became a Grandmaster in Sugar" that summarizes and spotlights the most significant points of my business life. I hope it will help illustrate my contributions to the industry and enable the reader to connect the dots about how hard I worked to rise to the level I did, which allowed me to even be considered for the award. With Brian O'Malley's permission, I will include his nomination letter.

I also decided to include a second appendix, "How I Became a US Chess Federation Life Master at Age Seventy". Like my incidents in the sugar industry, my chess anecdotes are scattered throughout the book. This second appendix will summarize my chess high points, of which I am quite proud.

Thank you for joining me on this journey—I hope you enjoyed it and learned some things along the way. If you've made it this far, humor an old man and read a little further. After that, go out in the world and do good work, practice unity, and live your life to the fullest. I promise you won't regret it.

APPENDIX A:
How I Became A Grandmaster in Sugar

I am told that, after age ninety, one is allowed to brag a little, and I thank my readers in advance for indulging me. Here is the nomination letter Brian O'Malley wrote about me for the Sugar Man of the Year Award:

November 1, 2022
B.W. Dyer and Company, LLC
Attention: Mr. Chip Dyer and Sugar Man of the Year (s) Committee

Dear Committee Members:

Please accept the following in nomination of Mr. Gene Salomon for Sugar Man of the Year (Nominated by Brian O'Malley, former very proud recipient).

*Many Major League Baseball Hall of Fame worthy candidates fall through the cracks and can only be properly recognized by the "Veterans Committee." In the Sugar Industry, such is the case with Gene Salomon. At **94 years young**, unbelievably he continues to consult and offer ideas to industry that are supportive of sugar interests in general, and edible molasses with specificity. His relentless determination can only serve to underscore a remarkable career and contribution to our sugar industry. Hopefully, the esteemed members of the committee can take on the additional role of a "Veteran's Committee" and recognize Gene for his many accomplishments, especially since there will be 2 awards next year due to the pandemic.*

Gene graduated from Havana University in 1953 with a 5-year degree in Agricultural Engineering and a 3-year degree in Sugar Technology. His first 7 years in the sugar industry were spent in Cuba. From 1953 until 1955 he was Chief Chemist and Manager of Agricultural Operations – Central Fe Sugar Mill in Las Villas, and from 1955 until 1960 as Plant Superintendent/Plant Manager of Providencia Sugar Mill in Havana. Concurrent with being Plant Manager, Gene was Professor of "Industrias Rurales" at Havana School of Agriculture and Sugar Chemical Engineering, also in Havana. (Many in the cane side of our industry spent formative years in Cuba. Without this influx of talent, our cane industry could never have developed so rapidly.)

In 1960, Gene joined Sucrest Corporation (which later became Ingredient Technology Corporation) in New York. He stayed there for 30 years and rose through the ranks:

- Research Chemist
- Process Research Engineer
- Assistant to the President
- Vice President Plant Operations
- President of Grandma Food Products, Canada
- President of ITC's largest division (Specialty Products)

In the late 60's and 70's, Gene helped organize and was President of the Animal Feed Group (Xtravim Division) and was responsible for the Blackstrap Molasses deep water terminals in Montreal, Hamilton, Dartmouth, Boston, and Wilmington. Under his strategic leadership, they converted all these facilities into Liquid Feed plants (molasses, urea plus minerals/vitamins). He also led the acquisition of the Calumet, IL liquid feed plant from Allied Chemical (now owned by ASR Group).

From 1982-1985 he served as Chairman, Board of Advisors, Rutgers University Food Science Department. Concurrently and until 1989, Gene was a member of the Board of Managers of the New Jersey Agricultural Experimentation Station.

From 1990-1994, Gene was employed by Florida Crystals and held positions as Vice President Central Romana (Dominican Republic), Vice President Osceola Farms and Vice President Okeelanta Sugar

Appendix A: How I Became A Grandmaster in Sugar

Corp. His specific areas of responsibility centered on New Business Development.

Eschewing the notion of retirement, Gene has spent the past 25+ years as a consultant to the sugar and food agribusiness industries, always with a focus on new business development. His clients have included:

- Florida Crystals
- Crompton & Knowles
- Complementos Alimenticios (Mexico)
- Crosby Molasses (not a client but a close and friendly advisor)
- La Abuela Carmen, Spain (currently consulting)

Gene lives in Lakewood, NJ with his wife Bea of 60+ years. They have 4 children: Gene, an entertainment industry lawyer in California; Maria, a schoolteacher in NJ; Henry, a mortgage industry professional in Texas; and Robert, a professor of International Business at The Stern School of Business, New York University.

Gene is recognized as a Chess Life Master, is a co-author of "40 Years of Friendship, 100 Games of Chess" (and is still capable of playing blindfolded)

I can personally attest to Gene's creativity and business deal-forming acumen that continues to produce ideas worthy of present-day commercial success. In short, Gene is a most worthy candidate for this prestigious award. Beyond his noteworthy lifelong contributions to the sugar industry, I am confident that Gene will inspire the audience with his passion about sugar and molasses specifically, and business deal-making skills in a more general sense. I would be honored to have my name alongside his as a recipient of Sugar Man of the Year.

Thank you to the distinguished members of the committee. I would be pleased to answer any questions about Gene Salomon's noteworthy career.

Sincerely,

Brian O'Malley (Former President, Domino Foods, Inc., and past Dyer Sugar Man of the Year)

Sweet Memories — Family, Friends, Chess, and Sugar

Brian did a wonderful job of summarizing the high points of my career, but there are so many events, anecdotes, and smaller details that shaped the trajectory of my career in the industry. I have already included a great many in the book and will try to avoid repetition as I relate some others.

After arriving in Cuba from Madrid in 1947, I traded my passion for chess from the 1940s in Spain for a new lifelong passion: *sugar*. It took me five arduous years at Havana University to get my degrees in agricultural engineering and in sugar technology while working full-time. After graduation in 1953, I began my career in the sugar industry there. The next seven years revolved around three *centrales* (sugar mills) in Cuba and the Dominican Republic.

Central Fe in Las Villas, Cuba, was my first one. In 1953, I became their agricultural research manager and chief chemist. That was my introduction to life on a sugar mill. I learned the sugar business, literally, from the ground up. I inspected the cane fields on horseback and shared the wonderful Cuban express coffee with the many noble *guajiros* (field workers) who lived and worked to turn San Benigno (the cane farm owned by Mr. Zulueta) into a center of agricultural experimentation. It was a wonderful experience, full of learning, and my work there generated true passion for the industry. However, the drive back to Havana was four hours each way, and I was missing my city and my friends, so I started looking for other opportunities. In 1956, after a fortuitous game of chess against my brother's friend, the friend recommended me for an open management position at a sugar mill much closer to Havana—only forty-five minutes away.

That was my second sugar mill, *Central Providencia*, in Havana. As plant superintendent there, I was in charge of manufacturing, and my eyes were opened to the wonderful world of "value-added" specialty products. We were the suppliers of Turbinado Sugars for the cereal giant Kellogg's, and Edible Molasses (also called cane juice molasses) for the American Molasses Company. The name "*Providencia*" turned out to be truer than I ever expected: I learned all about cane juice molasses (CJM) there, and the connection I made with American Molasses (who did business with *Central Providencia*) led directly to my first job in the US a few years later.

Appendix A: How I Became A Grandmaster in Sugar

In 1960, after moving to the US, I was hired by the soon-to-be Sucrest Corporation, who needed me to develop a new source of supply for their CJM. After visiting several potential suppliers in different countries, I selected *Central Romana* in the Dominican Republic—my third *Central*. I could never, ever have suspected that my association with Romana, which began in December 1961, could enrich my life so much, and that I would continue to be quite actively associated with them until 2001…and beyond! My time there was memorable, not only for the lasting friendships I made but also for its R&D content and several months of extended "on-the-job" honeymoon! Those 1961–1962 honeymoon days were just the beginning of many new experiences. I worked with CJM in *Central Providencia* in Cuba in the mid-'50s, *Central Romana* in the Dominican Republic in 1961, and later, *Central Madre Tierra* in Guatemala in 1994!

Back at Sucrest, a colleague and I developed a program to reduce sugar losses during the refining process by closely monitoring the residual flows of water drainage and adding an "Auto-Analyzer" for continuous monitoring. To my knowledge, we were the first sugar refinery to use this equipment, and I remember that Refined Sugars from Yonkers, New York, followed our lead a few months later. The Auto-Analyzer did help us to reduce losses significantly, and the program was most successful.

1963 was an exceptional year—I was promoted to assistant to the president at the Sucrest Corporation. My responsibilities increased but still included being responsible for the contract with *Central Romana* and the molasses operations in Louisiana. At the same time, I was involved with other sugar and molasses projects with the Dominican government-owned sugar mills. Later that year, I was also offered a very lucrative vice president position at *Central Romana*, but since we had two young children, I politely declined. (Besides that, I was happy at my job, and the future looked promising.) However, I gave them the name of an excellent candidate who they eventually hired—Carlos Morales Troncoso. Carlos then hired Eduardo Martinez Lima and Raul Perdomo for his team at Romana, and my friendship with both men was born. (Little did I know that my connection to both Carlos and

Martinez Lima would figure so prominently in my career twenty-plus years later!)

Shortly after being promoted to assistant to the president, there was a supply problem in the market of blackstrap molasses used for livestock feed. It escalated to a worlwide crisis and left our blackstrap molasses deep water terminals (Dartmouth, Montreal, Boston, and Wilmington) without supplies. I contacted my old friends in the sugar industry, and one of them, in Venezuela, said he could get blackstrap molasses for me from the Vollmer brothers' sugar mill but that Venezuela did not have storage tanks in their ports for shipment via tankers. Our head of shipping confirmed this but pointed out that since Venezuela is a petroleum country, there were several fleets of tanker trucks that could be used to transport the molasses to the port. They would then be transferred into portable tanks that we would place at the dock, and with rented pumping equipment, we could load several thousand tons on the tanker. The process took several days, which brought additional costs, but fortunately, the vendor of the molasses was interested in finding new markets for his products and was happy to cooperate with us. That is how we succeeded in helping Venezuela make its first export ever of blackstrap molasses to the United States.

In addition to the operation in Venezuela, I actually also solved our company's blackstrap molasses supply crisis a second time, this time in the Dominican Republic. Until then, we had not been an approved buyer since the Dominican Republic historically sold only to the three major world molasses companies—United Molasses (and Pacific Molasses), National Molasses, and Industrial Molasses. I began to work on a possible purchase (via back channels) through an old friend, Urbano Martinez, advisor and friend to Juan Bosch, the president of the Dominican Republic. Urbano arranged a meeting for us with President Bosch, Sucrest President Frank Staples, and Senior Vice President Harold Saufley. After a brief, terrifying hiccup with the meeting location, we met and were able to arrange our company's first purchase of several thousand tons of Dominican blackstrap molasses from the government-owned sugar mills.

After rapid promotions from the research side to the operations area, first as assistant to the president and shortly thereafter to vice president of plant operations, I became a world traveler in the 1960s and 1970s, beginning with 1963 trip to Tate & Lyle in the UK (which eventually resulted in the birth of our candy fondant, Nulofond, and a subsequent cross-licensing agreement with C&H). Another benefit of that trip was my initial contact with United Molasses, then a subsidiary of Tate & Lyle.

In addition to the annual February trips to Barbados to negotiate the purchasing contract, there were three marvelous cities that I visited every year: New Orleans, Montreal, and Santo Domingo. In New Orleans, I was responsible for the operation of the old Colonial Molasses plant right in the city (North Gayoso Street). I also had to visit the (then) five sugar mills producing edible molasses as I was in charge of the company's procurement program. Montreal was the home of Sucrest's Canadian subsidiary and most profitable product line, Grandma Molasses. As a vice president of Sucrest, I had the responsibility for their Canadian operations and had to visit the old Notre Dame Street plant periodically. (At one point in the 1970s, I narrowly rescued Grandma Molasses from being sold to Duffy-Mott as part of a larger deal.)

The 1980s

The first half of the 1980s were exceptional years in my life as an executive for Ingredient Technology Corporation (ITC), successor to Sucrest. After the president of the largest division of the company (Specialty Products) announced his impending retirement, I was put in charge of those operations in addition to continuing as head of my division, Xtravim, which specialized in animal feed. Suddenly, my group (Specialty Products and Xtravim) became the most important in the company, and I began to develop new businesses that took me to Europe frequently. It was common for me to visit Paris, Marseille, London, Frankfurt, Milan, or Zurich with the idea of opening new markets for our ingredients in the pharmaceutical or nutraceutical industry, or to secure supplies of malt extract from England or Italy. My frequent traveling allowed me to not only make new friends but to also stay in contact with many old friends as well.

My friendship with Carlos Morales Troncoso (vice president at *Central Romana*, among other titles) had continued for years. Around 1985, he was trying to form a group to purchase *Central Romana* from Gulf & Western. I had offered to arrange a meeting with my company, ITC, to explore the possibility of cooperation, but Carlos called and said he had already met with a Florida group headed by Alfy Fanjul and that it looked promising. My last meeting with Carlos was a few years later. As vice president of the Dominican Republic and a sugar industry leader on his own, he was the guest speaker at the yearly Sugar Club dinner in New York. After the end of the speech, several of us were in line to shake hands with him. To everyone's surprise (including my own), when my turn came up, he did not shake my hand but gave me a big "*abrazo*"—one of those hugs reserved for close friends.

Black Monday, 1987

One Monday, in 1987, I was traveling to Switzerland for ITC. I had a new Swiss customer for whom we had developed Edible Molasses flakes for the nutraceutical market, and we were going to explore other new ingredients and/or joint business. Rudy Everstadt, president of ITC, was joining me, and we had arranged a dinner meeting with our client in Zurich. While I was flying from Madrid (after a weekend family visit), and Rudy was on his way from London, the New York Stock Market crashed. It was Black Monday of 1987; our stock had dropped from $21 a share to $13, and we presumed we were going to be the target of an unfriendly takeover attempt. We canceled all the meetings and headed back to NY to figure out how to protect ourselves—a seven-hour trip of intense discussion. I suggested to Rudy (and he agreed) that an ideal "white knight" to come to our rescue would be Alfy Fanjul. His group, Flo-Sun, had the available capital for an acquisition, we were already doing business with one of his companies (*Central Romana*), and therefore, ITC might be attractive to them.

Back in Manhattan, I called Eduardo Martinez Lima, one of Alfy's VPs (who I had met twenty years earlier when Morales Troncoso hired him for *Central Romana*) and asked if he could arrange a meeting with

Alfy to explore the idea. He said sure, and the meeting was scheduled for a couple of weeks later in November.

Three days before the meeting, Rudy called me. We had received an official tender offer to buy the company from Malt Products, a corporate rival, so Rudy could not participate in the meeting with Alfy and Flo-Sun. He asked me to go alone and tone down the meeting, so I flew to Palm Beach and changed the presentation to say that we were "looking for new opportunities/and/or partnerships." Unfortunately, nothing came out of the meeting, and we hired an investment firm to explore alternative offers. The eventual winner was Crompton & Knowles, with an offer of $29 per share.

In 1988, after thirty successful years at Sucrest//ITC, the company was acquired by Crompton & Knowles, which was much larger. It is popularly believed that when you get to your sixties, you cannot wait to retire, but that was not how I felt. I enjoyed my work; retirement was not foremost in my mind, but I did not know what to expect. Fortunately, I was protected by a "golden parachute," a type of contract given to key executives to provide assurance that even if the company is taken over, they will be protected by a separation contract.

Crompton & Knowles convinced me not to retire yet, to instead wait two years. They also asked me to continue in charge of the division that I currently led in order to aid in the transition and even expanded my responsibilities to make me feel wanted. They assured me that my compensation check would still be waiting for me at the end of those two years, and I would have the option to retire or continue in my position. The proposal was interesting; so, at age sixty, I negotiated a new contract. However, I did not care for the new corporate management style and decided to make a change.

In 1989, I began teaching Mike DeLuca (my financial VP and a friend from Sucrest in the '70s) the ins and outs of the business so he could take over. I brought him on the February trip to Barbados to meet Jim Crosby and planted an idea: the possibility of selling the Grandma Molasses retail product line to Crosby with a long-term supply contract for the cane juice molasses. (It took several years for that idea to come to fruition, but today, Grandma Molasses in Canada is a market leader for the Crosby group.) Since that was the same year that Fancy Molasses decided to stop producing their molasses, the annual Crosby and ITC February trip to Barbados that year turned into a farewell dinner with our friends from Barbados Fancy Molasses and our Canadian friends of Crosby Molasses.

That same year, my old friend Eduardo Martinez Lima (who knew I was considering leaving or retiring) told me that Alfy Fanjul was willing to hire me as a VP of Okeelanta, to become the next general manager. I politely declined since I was still under contract with C&K but thanked Eduardo for his help. A few months later, Eduardo called me again; this time, to tell me that they were thinking of creating a new position to help Flo-Sun sugar mills develop new business. He asked if I was interested, and I definitely was. I started working for Alfy at Flo-Sun in 1990, at age sixty-two, as vice president of Okeelanta Sugar Company and Osceola Farms in Florida, and…vice president of *Central Romana* in the Dominican Republic! Things had come full circle—VP of *Central Romana* was the job I had turned down almost thirty years earlier in 1963!

After a few months of visiting the plants and interviewing key personnel, I proposed four areas of new business development.

1. Become an independent refinery and enter the field of "value-added sugar specialties."
2. Expand the Sem-Chi Rice Mill operation with emphasis on organic rice products.
3. Start a joint R&D program with IFF for natural flavoring aromatics from cane sugar.
4. Investigate new technologies for further sugar recovery from molasses.

That first proposal was, by far, the most major. Luis Fernandez, one of Alfy's top managers, had suggested the same thing and was already working with a consultant. This resulted in an instant alliance between us, and we worked doggedly on the proposal. Luis and I had been working on our pet project for several months when, one day, when I thought that we were ready to celebrate, Luis walked from his office into mine (just ten feet across the hall), closed the door, and told me: "Gene, we just lost our battle."

Apparently, a group of three to four executives, including the influential corporate lawyer, had just returned in the corporate jet from a meeting at Savannah, where they had obtained significant concessions in the terms of the contract. After a pregnant silence, following this bitter, disappointing news, I remember asking: "Luis, could you ask Alfy in my name if we could have a meeting to present our case?" His reply: "Yes, Gene. That I can do. Yes, I can." A few days later, we all were on the way to Casa de Campo in *Central Romana* to meet Alfy for a final decision-making meeting.

After several people presented their points of view, Alfy pointedly asked me a question I will never forget: "Gene, let's imagine that tomorrow, we start selling our refined sugar, and Savannah reduces their selling prices dramatically in our territory. What is the result?" It was a very good question…and frankly, I believe that my answer was even better: "Alfy, we may lose one million dollars and Savannah will lose ten million." After a brief pause, Alfy decided to go the independent route. I believe that the success that followed, selling our own brand, "Florida Crystals" refined sugar, was the true beginning of the company's growth (via acquisitions) several years later. Today, admiring the refined sugar world giant that Luis Fernandez and Alfy created (ASR Group), I feel proud just remembering my initial participation in the original decision to start selling our own refined sugar production under our own brand. With a smile of satisfaction, I remember the next two years working as a team with Luis to organize the startup. It was indeed an exciting project, which opened the door to future acquisitions of sugar refining companies and to becoming a world leader in "value-added" specialty sugar products.

I was able to help the Florida Crystals group for many years, beyond even my three years as an executive and four as a consultant. I also assisted them by securing supplies of cane juice molasses from Latin America as a consultant for Domino years later and by assisting Luis Fernandez to recruit my old "right hand," Mike DeLuca, to organize their new natural and organic ingredients business. We also worked together in developing new opportunities in the area of spray-dried sweeteners (honey, malt, and molasses) in cooperation with a Mexican company (*Complementos Alimenticios*) for whom I consulted for years. Remarkably, I had introduced the key executives of the Mexican group to Mike DeLuca back in 1984, shortly after hiring him as my financial VP at ITC Specialty Products. I am truly proud of how Mike grew our original Specialty Products—ITC group! My relationship with Luis and Mike DeLuca continued for many years as friends, and I was able to occasionally help them in the specialty products business world by organizing cooperative programs with some of my other clients.

My second recommendation for future growth involved Sem-Chi, a tiny rice mill. At my suggestion, we increased the planting and the mill capacity to triple the volume within the first couple of years, and Mike DeLuca accelerated the growth in the following years.

The most fascinating program (in its success and failures) was a seven-year R&D contract I negotiated with IFF only months after joining the Flo-Sun group in 1990. The contract included a pilot plant designed and financed by IFF to be installed at Osceola Farms to identify and extract natural flavoring ingredients from cane sugar. The technical direction was by two exceptional researchers. The first year of the contract, Allen Pittet, one of the researchers, discovered a natural source of DMS (dimethyl sulfide), which, at the time, had a market value of several hundred dollars per kilogram, and we had a few other ideas in the works. It was a real discovery: We became the first sugar company in the world to produce natural DMS!

Late in 1993, as my contract with Flo-Sun was about to expire, I sat down with Alfy to explain that, for family reasons, I had to return to New Jersey and was going to retire. At the time, the sales of DMS were significant—over $100,000 per year—and I believe that Alfy was impressed with my results. We still had four years on our contract with IFF, so he asked me if I would be willing to continue in charge of the program as a dedicated consultant. That was the beginning of my "new career," which lasted for the next thirty years.

As part of that career, I was able to help Florida Crystals on other projects, which resulted in Domino adding CJM to their product line. (Memories from the mid-'50s, alive in the late-1990s.)

Appendix A: How I Became A Grandmaster in Sugar

In the mid-1990s, Crompton & Knowles decided to sell its sugar specialty product business. At the time, I was consulting for both companies; so, we had a meeting with Mike De Luca (VP of C&K) and Luis Fernandez (Florida Crystals) at the Manhattan office of Salomon Brothers to explore the possibility of an acquisition. I remember with a smile on my face that as every participant introduced himself, when my turn came, I said: "I'm not sure if I'm here because I was once a VP of C&K, and another time a VP at Florida Crystals, or just because my last name is *Salomon*."

A few years later, shortly after the Fanjul group acquired the Domino Sugar company, Brian O'Malley became the new company president. I made a point to congratulate him and learned that his boss, Luis Fernandez, had suggested to him that I could probably be of great help to him as a consultant in the area of "value-added products." Brian put me in touch with "Cele" Ruiz, who at the time was in charge of the Specialty Products group at Domino. Cele and I visited the Chalmette Sugar refinery in New Orleans, and then flew to Mexico, to introduce him to my friend and client, Felipe Suberbie, head of "*Complementos Alimenticios*."

At just about that same time, I got a call from Julio Asensio, head of the "Madre Tierra" Sugar Mill in Guatemala. Julio explained to me that C&K had sold the business to a European company, and they were having some difficulties. His question: Could I help him to get a new, reliable customer? (Ironically, as a consultant a few years earlier, I had helped to design and start up a "cane juice molasses" plant there after negotiating a long-term supply contract with my client Crompton & Knowles.) I invited Julio to fly to Newark to meet with Brian in Iselin…and the rest is history.

Finally, as I finish this book at age ninety-four, I am working on my last consulting project. (I guess I really do not understand the concept of retirement.) I am helping my friend Manuel Vaquero Ortiz, head of *La Abuela Carmen* (the European leader in the black garlic industry), to develop some products, including edible molasses. The many connections and friendships I have made over my seventy years in the industry have always been a large factor in my success, and I am most grateful for them. In the same way that longevity and success in

215

chess earn a player the title of Chess Master, I believe that my seventy years in the sugar industry, and the many games I have played and won on the "black-and-white board of sugar and molasses", have earned me the right to consider myself a "Sugar Grandmaster". It is a title I like very much.

APPENDIX B:
US Chess Federation Life Master at Age 70, Chess Writer at 89

Longevity is perhaps my only claim to fame in chess. I have gone from being a tournament player in 1943 to a chess writer eighty years later in 2023. During those years, I enjoyed many wonderful experiences revolving around chess. I feel honored that many complimentary articles have been written about me over the years, and I am proud of the books I have written (or co-written) about my chess adventures. I initially wanted to include some of my most significant games in this book, but this is primarily a book about family. All my games are available in other books, articles, or chess databases, so I decided to refer any chess-loving readers to those places.

My first book, *40 Years of Friendship: 100 Games of Chess,* was written in 2014 with my chess buddies Steve Pozarek and Wayne Conover. This book details our friendship, which began at the Westfield Chess Club and has grown over the last several decades, and includes one hundred games selected from our tournaments.

My second book, *Jugando en el tablero de la vida,* written with co-author Javier Cordero and published in 2022 in Spain by *Chessy,* is a comprehensive, chess-focused biographical book. Aside from being my co-author, Javier maintains an excellent website about Spanish chess—*Historia del ajedrez español* (http://www.historiadelajedrezespanol.es). He has graciously dedicated a page in the *Articulos* section to me, where many of the articles I have written for various publications can be found in English and Spanish.

Javier honors me with this description of my life: "*Gene Salomon* was one of the most promising youngsters in the Spanish chess scene of the 1940s. Circumstances of life did not permit him to fulfill his potential. He left Spain in 1947 to relocate in his mother's birth country—Cuba, where he had to abandon chess due to the pressures of having to work while going to Havana University Engineering School. In 1960, Gene left Cuba for the US. In 1968, after sixteen years of complete absence from the chess world, he returned to the tournament circuit, where he never reached the original expectations but still had a new thirty-year career with some colorful experiences. His surfacing in Spain in 2016 through the social press was a surprise. Putting together his rich history was a pleasant task. We were able to launch the project thanks to the book that Eugene and his two "chess buddies" (Wayne Conover and Steve Pozarek) wrote under the title: 40 Years of Friendship: 100 Games of Chess. The original book (both as an eBook and under the* Forward Chess *format) was written in English. With the authors' permission, we translated it into Spanish so that we could publish it through the Internet for the benefit of our readers."*

The essence of my chess life was also described by Miguel Angel Nepomuceno in the five articles he published in *Zenda/libros* reflecting our interview in Madrid in April 2017. His opening sentence made me proud: "The protagonist of this story is not a Grandmaster, although he has defeated a few. Nor is he a professional chess player. As the North Americans would say it, Eugenio Salomón Rugarcía is an authentic *self-made-man…*"

I wrote my first article about chess as a teenager in 1946, which was published by *Ajedrez Espanol.* Seventy years later, inspired by my friend Miguel Angel, I picked up the pen again, and wrote articles for the monthly British magazine, *Chess,* the annual New Jersey Chess Federation magazine, *Atlantic Chess News,* and, more recently, the quarterly *Chess Journalists of America* newsletter. I could never have guessed that the first article in 1946 would lead to me being an author of a book in 2023 at age ninety-four.

For those readers interested in chess, these articles are all available on my page at Javier Cordero's website, *Historia del ajedrez español,* which can be accessed at http://www.historiadelajedrezespanol.es/articulos/salomon_eng.htm. On my page, the reader may enjoy most of the articles (which include some of my best games) in English and Spanish.

As a conclusion to this Appendix B, and with permission from editor Richard Palliser of the magazine, I will copy the two-page article published in the prestigious magazine *Chess* of London (www.chess.co.uk) in January 2020, titled "Chess for Life". I felt particularly honored to have been published in this magazine because I had interacted with its founder, B.H. Wood, back in the 1940s in my native Gijón.

Sweet Memories — Family, Friends, Chess, and Sugar

Chess for Life

Even at 91 years old, BH Wood's former opponent from his trips to northern Spain, Eugene Salomon, still likes to play not just chess, but also bridge

One year ago, the day before my 90th birthday, I wrote: "90 Years of Coincidences, that's what life has been: 19 years in my native Spain, 13 years in Cuba, and 58 years in the good, old USA. A chess passion of 75 years and a 65-year career in business. Reflecting about tomorrow, when I will become 90 years old, I realize that I'm just a drop of water in the large ocean of immigrants that die any given day, proud of their heritage and equally as proud of the legacy they leave behind – in my case, four children and seven grandchildren."

A few weeks ago my friend Luis Mendez Castedo sent me a copy of the September CHESS, in which he and his brother Pedro, co-authors of *The Gijón International Tournaments 1944-1965*, wrote: "The book has been enriched by a foreword from Eugene Salomon, the living legend of Spanish chess and the last survivor of the 1947 Gijón tournament."

No, I do not pretend to be a legend; I just had the fortune of having three true legends as my chess teachers: my father (my first teacher, my 'hero'), my uncle and chess poet Dr. Rugarcia, and the chess genius of all time, Alexander Alekhine, who so much helped me with his wise advise about chess and life.

A few weeks after returning from a 'memory lane' trip to Madrid and Gijón (the birthplace of my chess career) this summer, I gave a lecture at the Toms River Chess Club, New Jersey, and as a follow-up, wrote an article about what I had learnt from my three chess teachers.

Then, reading in these pages about 'Mr. Chess', BH Wood, brought a lot of memories about the IV Gijón International in which we both participated. Moreover, the last time I had seen this publication was exactly 72 years ago when the September 1947 issue contained an article with a photograph of BH Wood, myself and the other 12 participants from Gijón, which I read in Madrid just a month before leaving for Havana.

I still conserve an original of that issue and reproduced the article in the Ebook I co-wrote with Steve Pozarek and Wayne Conover: *40 Years of Friendship – 100 Games of Chess*. That September 1947 issue of *Chess* has travelled with me from Madrid to Havana to New York, and it's now here in my home in the company of the chess pieces that Alekhine used at Gijón in 1944.

Nowadays I like to write and I settled on the above title because a few years after retiring from competitive chess, at the age of 70, I

Eugene Salomon is still going strong at the age of 91, pictured here at his local Tom Rivers Chess Club in New Jersey. Eugene is hoping to again play in the legendary U.S. Amateur Team Championship next month, an event which attracts well over a thousand players each year.

discovered in Duplicate Bridge a good way to continue cultivating my competitive spirit. Moreover, I realised at the same time, just as you can find true poetry in chess combinations, the same pleasurable sensation when you learn how to exploit the 'distributional value' of the hands you have been dealt.

Back to the main subject, chess at 17 and at 70, and here is one of my favourite games which I won as a teenager.

J.M.Fuentes-E.Salomon
Madrid 1946
Ruy Lopez

1 e4 e5 2 ♘f3 ♘c6 3 ♗b5 a6 4 ♗a4 ♘f6
5 ♕e2 b5 6 ♗b3 ♗e7 7 ♗d5 ♘xd5
8 exd5 ♘b4 9 ♕e4? ♗b7 10 ♘c3 0-0

11 ♗d1? f5 12 ♕xe5 ♗f6 13 ♕f4 ♗xc3
14 bxc3 ♘xd5 15 ♕d4 d6 16 ♖e1 c5

17 ♕h4 ♘xc3+! 0-1

Appendix B: US Chess Federation Life Master at Age 70, Chess Writer at 89

Completing the powerplay. 18 dxc3 ♗xf3+ picks up the white queen

This and plenty more games can be found in the aforementioned Ebook, including the way I ground down John Watson at the 1996 World Open, as well as the following effort.

E.Salomon-L.Murzin
World Open, Philadelphia 1998
Catalan Opening

1 d4 ♘f6 2 c4 e6 3 g3 d5 4 ♗f3 ♗e7 5 ♗g2 0-0 6 0-0 dxc4 7 ♕a4 a6 8 ♕xc4 b5 9 ♕c2 ♗b7 10 ♗f4 ♗d6 11 ♘bd2 ♘bd7 12 ♘g5 ♗xf4 13 gxf4 ♕xg2 14 ♔xg2 c5 15 dxc5 ♘xc5 16 ♖fd1 ♕e7 17 b4 ♘a4 18 ♘de4 g6 19 ♖ac1 ♘d5 0 e3 ♕xb4?

21 ♖xd5! exd5 22 ♘f6+ ♔g7 23 ♕c7 ♕b2 24 ♘xd5 ♖ac8? 25 ♕e7 ♖xc1 26 ♘e6+ ♔h6 27 ♕g5# 1-0

Eugene meets Garry Kasparov and impresses the great man by showing him a photo of himself and one of his chess heroes, Alekhine.

Whether readers are curious enough to check out my other games or not, I certainly want to share one of the most emotional game of my life, which was analysed in depth by my opponent. It was half a century ago when my first chess teacher and hero, my father, passed away at the end of January 1968. I had been retired from chess for 13 years (eight in Cuba while I enjoyed an exciting professional career, and another eight in the U.S creating a new business career and, most importantly, starting a family).

All of a sudden I felt the need to play chess again. Why? I will never know, but there was a strong inspirational force and I played with a mental intensity I had never felt before or since. I entered the New Jersey State Open and my first game was against one of the strongest youngsters in the state, Steve Pozarek, who recalls:

"In 1968, I was an 18-year-old chess player with an Expert rating and ambitions of becoming a Master, and, just before the beginning of my sophomore year in college, I entered the New Jersey Open. My opponent in the first round was Unrated, meaning that the player had not played in any rated tournaments (in the US!) and was usually very inexperienced at chess. It hardly seemed like a very fateful moment, but as I recently read, 'Fate would not have the reputation it has if it simply did what it seemed it would do.'

"In my youthful enthusiasm, I missed some of the indications that my opponent was no ordinary Unrated player. First of all, he wasn't a young kid; he was a serious looking man in his 30s or 40s. Second, he kept score of the game, not in the usual American notation, but in a language I did not quite understand. Finally, he moved the pieces with a confidence of someone who has done it many, many times before.

"Ignoring these warning signs, I opened as White with the Queen Pawn, something I almost never did at the time. When he defended with the King's Indian Defense, I countered with the Saemisch Variation, a line that I had never played before (and have never played since!). After all, what was the harm? He was Unrated.

"As early as moves 8 through 10, my opponent maneuvered his two Knights in a way that seemed unusual to me. I think I took it as further evidence of his inexperience, but in fact it was a clear indication of my unfamiliarity with the nuances of the position. Very soon after that I realized that I was getting into trouble. Flustered with the sudden change in events, I played several moves without purpose, while my opponent powerfully realigned his pieces. By move 26, I was two pawns down and my position was collapsing on all fronts. My resignation at that point was probably the only time in my life that it came as a disappointment to the player on the other side of the board. My 'inexperienced' and unrated opponent had calculated a very pretty checkmate in 5 moves that I had not allowed him to demonstrate in the game.

"And that is how I met my lifelong friend Gene Salomon! As I pouted after the game, Gene consoled my father (also a very good chess player) with the information that although Unrated in the US, he had been a strong Master both in Spain and in Cuba. The only reason that he didn't have a USCF rating was that he had not played in any tournaments in the United States since his arrival in this country some 10 years earlier. He had not played in any tournaments at all in over 15 years. However, in that NJ Open, Gene went on over the next 5 rounds to contend for the NJ State title, losing out only in the final round when an unfortunate misunderstanding about the schedule forced him to play without sufficient time. He achieved a provisional rating of USCF Master as a result (a title it took me over 10 more years to earn)."

S.Pozarek-E.Salomon
New Jersey Open 1968
King's Indian Defence

1 c4 ♘f6 2 ♘c3 g6 3 e4 d6 4 d4 ♗g7 5 f3 0-0 6 ♗e3 e5 7 d5 a5 8 ♗d3 ♘a6 9 ♘ge2 ♘d7 10 ♕d2 ♘b4 11 0-0 f5 12 exf5 gxf5 13 f4 ♘xd3 14 ♕xd3 e4 15 ♕d2 ♘c5 16 ♗d4 ♕e7 17 ♗xg7 ♔xg7 18 ♘b5 ♖f7 19 ♘ed4 ♘d3 20 b3 ♗d7 21 ♕e3 ♖c8 22 a3 ♖f6 23 b4?! c6 24 ♘c3 ♖g6 25 ♘ce2? cxd5 26 ♘g3 ♖xc4! 0-1

And the finish I had been hoping to execute? The idea was 27 ♘dxf5 ♗xf5 28 ♘xf5 ♖xg2+ 29 ♔h1 ♖cc2! 30 ♘xg7 ♖xh2+ 31 ♔g1 ♖cg2#.

You might also be wondering how I thought sharing that game would serve as a homage to my father and to my love of chess? I certainly have a debt of gratitude for all the ways in which chess has enriched my life, from bonding with my father to bonding with my sons to precious friendships to invaluable lessons about reasoning, so important in business and in life.

I must mention too that my father was a volunteer who fought with the British forces against Hitler. When he insisted in playing chess with me every night back in 1942, he would talk to me between games about life and his experiences. I will never forget all about his fighting the Nazis as a volunteer in the British Army prior to Dunkirk, as well as his subsequent journey, escaping Hitler to return to Spain. It is a story about how the winds of life blow us from place to place – just a leaf in the storm, as Lin Yutang would say.

And, finally, in February I hope to play as part of a team of 'super seniors' in the U.S Amateur Team Tournament, which usually contains over 1,300 players and will again be run by my good friend Steve Doyle who has now been at the helm for 30 years. Chess truly does continue to enrich our lives.

Ed. – If youu would like to read more from Eugene, do check out his articles at www.historiadelajedrezespanol.es/articulos/salomon_eng.htm

Acknowledgments

I owe so much to so many family members and friends that I will surely forget someone—my apologies in advance to everyone!

On the Salomon side of the family, I received information, historical documents, and pictures from Ralph (grandson of my Uncle Paul) about the family in Australia, and from Dani (Uncle Max's grandson) from Mexico.

The information I received from the families of my father's first cousins, who I first met sixty-plus years ago and still remain in contact with, was remarkable. Peter Joseph, son of Cousin Rudy, was a most influential factor in my converting this book from a chess autobiography into a true family history, full of bittersweet memories and lessons for my grandchildren.

On the Schwarz side of my father's family, I am grateful to Annette Woolf for the information about our great-aunt who died in a concentration camp in Germany. This came as a complete surprise to me, impacted me deeply, and, hopefully, adds value to the message in this book.

On my mother's side of the family, Luis Rugarcía (son of my cousin Miguel) from Seville, supplied me with historical information and old photos of the Rugarcía family, and Teresina (Maria Teresa Marino Menendez, daughter of my cousin Teté who lives in Gijón) was a source of information about the Menendez Rugarcía family.

A huge thank you must also be given to someone who enriched the book with his descriptions of the times of my life in which he was a main character, my nephew Roberto Moriyón. Roberto narrated how our lives and paths crossed over a chessboard from the Canary Islands to Princeton University. (He was also my partner in bridge tournaments over the internet and whenever I visited Spain.)

I would also like to remember some special friends from my professional life: Brian O'Malley (for whom I consulted when he was the head of Domino), for his many years of friendship and for honoring me with his kind nomination for a prestigious industry award. I also want to thank Mike DeLuca, who, for the later parts of my life related to edible molasses, was my right hand in many of my adventures and successes. Our friendship started in the late 1970s and continues today. I enjoyed him considering me his mentor, and I admire his tremendous contribution to the specialty sugars business.

My special gratitude to Steve Pozarek and Wayne Conover (my co-authors of *40 Years of Friendship, 100 Games of Chess*) with whom I still have monthly gatherings celebrating our 50 years of friendship, which began when we were chess teammates. Steve Pozarek, under the influence of fifty years of friendship, wrote a kind and heartfelt article about the first game we played in 1968 titled, "The Best Game I Ever Lost."

My deepest thanks also to Steve Shoshin, president of the Toms River Chess Club, and Steve Doyle, past president of the US Chess Federation and past vice-president of FIDE. "The two Steves" welcomed me into the Toms River Chess Club, invited me to give lectures and simultaneous exhibitions, and inducted me into the Toms River Chess Club Hall of Fame along with world champions. What a huge honor!

I am also grateful to three chess writers and historians: Javier Cordero, my co-author for the Spanish book and an artist of narration who helped me organize my memories; and Miguel Ángel Nepomuceno, my "forever friend", who interviewed me six years ago for the articles he wrote for *Zenda/libros*. It was he who planted the seed of this book in my brain by telling me that the variety of experiences that my father and I lived was a compelling story that had to be shared; and finally, Luis Méndez Castedo, for whom I had the pleasure of being a living witness for his book about the international tournaments in Gijón, recently published in English. The process helped me to remember, and almost relive, the beautiful era of my chess in Spain in the 1940s.

I felt honored to have him write the prologue to my book *Jugando en el tablero de la vida*.

I would like to give thanks to my sister Ana María, of Majadahonda, Madrid, who helped me remember several stories from my childhood, like how she used to call the famous Spanish General Miaja "Tío Pepe" as a child before the Spanish Civil War, or when she grabbed my hand to run into a doorway while a German *Stuka* (bomber aircraft) machine-gunned the street as we walked down the *Paseo de Begoña*.

Most importantly, I want to thank my wonderful wife, Bea, for her unbelievable patience with me while writing this book, and our children and grandchildren for being a constant source of inspiration and pride. Thank you all for your love and support. To all those family members and friends I have not mentioned, I am truly grateful for your help and for enriching my life.

The authors wish to extend an enormous *thank you* to our outstanding cover designer, Joe Schwartz (who has been friends with Diane and the Salomon family for many years) for his time and talented contributions to this book. At the most hectic point in the school year, Joe exhibited extraordinary patience with us, and created a cover design that incorporated all of Gene's wishes. This is Joe's second cover for a Salomon family book, and we are very grateful to him. We also wish to thank Joshua M. Anderson, Martha Bullen of Bullen Publishing Services, and Andrea Vanryken of Yellow Bird Editors for their guidance and help in making this important book as perfect as possible.

About the Authors

J. Eugene "Gene" Salomon was born in Spain in 1928 and is thrilled to be publishing this book in time for his 95th birthday.

Gene is a devoted family man, and has been married to Bea, his Brooklyn angel, for sixty-two years. Together, they are the proud parents of four, and grandparents of seven. Gene makes it a priority to stay in touch with all his relatives all over the world, especially his close family in Spain.

Gene was among the best chess players in Spain and Cuba in the late 1940s and early 1950s. After many years away from chess, he earned the U.S Chess Federation rating as a Life Master at age 70. He also received a Silver Life Master Certificate from the American Contract Bridge League at age 93.

Gene earned degrees in Sugar Technology and Agricultural Engineering at Havana University. He is known as one of the foremost experts in the world on the subject of edible molasses and has traveled extensively in his work. Gene's resumé includes significant contributions to the sugar industry, and he has been nominated for the Dyer Award, the "Sugar Man of the Year." He is still working as a consultant in new business development in the food industry.

The publication date, July 18th, is a significant date for Gene: July 18, 1936 was the start of the Spanish Civil War, and July 18, 1960 was the date of the Castro speech that convinced Gene to leave Cuba. On July 18th, 2023, he leaves this book to his seven grandchildren as his legacy.

Sweet Memories — Family, Friends, Chess, and Sugar

Diane S. Dahl is excited to make her literary debut as a published author with *Sweet Memories*. She grew up in Old Bridge, New Jersey, where she first met the Salomon family 45 years ago.

Diane has always been a lover of words and language. She began learning Spanish, Italian, and American Sign Language (ASL) in high school and college and has long been involved with the local Ministry with the Deaf as an interpreter.

Diane holds a B.A. in Spanish and Elementary/Special Education and a Master's degree in Literacy from Rutgers University. Her professional career includes thirty-one years in a predominantly Spanish-speaking urban New Jersey school district as an elementary special educator, reading specialist, and supervisor of special services. Diane applied her skills and fascination with language to accelerate her students' reading acquisition and to improve literacy instruction for all. Diane used her Spanish daily not only to communicate, but also to help her students improve their literacy skills in order to become fluent readers. This tremendously rewarding passion brought her great joy. She retired in 2021, but has recently "unretired" to teach struggling readers at the high school level.

In her spare time, Diane enjoys scrapbooking, tracing her family's ancestry, collecting Willy Wonka memorabilia, and having adventures with her family and their friends, the Gamers. She sends tons of love and gratitude to her amazing family— her husband Diedrick, and their daughters, Elizabeth and Victoria, for their constant patience, support, assistance, and love, especially over the last two years while she was immersed in working on this book.

www.ingramcontent.com/pod-product-compliance
Lightning Source LLC
LaVergne TN
LVHW010201070526
838199LV00062B/4440